View from Section 26

A fan's look at the minor leagues featuring pro
hockey's most unwanted team

by Curtis Walker

View from Section 26

Table of Contents

To the few.

The embarrassed.

The Moose fans.

Introduction

I was one of the few fans who closely followed the fortunes of the Manitoba Moose, a minor-league hockey team that played in the International Hockey League (IHL) for five seasons before moving to the American Hockey League (AHL).

The Moose replaced the Jets of the National Hockey League (NHL), who had moved to Phoenix following 24 seasons in Winnipeg. I would be one of the few former Jets fans to transfer my allegiance to the Moose and, over the next eight years, I would be in for a veritable potpourri of previously unimaginable sights and sounds that would transform game day into a vaudeville show. New phrases were about to enter my vernacular: puck bunny, token adult, human bowling, Bubba the Smoker, Chateau Riendeau, turkey curling, chicken challenge and Schnooky.

The Moose would use the slogan that hockey didn't leave, it just got closer to home. Unlike many marketing slogans, this one would prove deadly accurate. It was truly hockey at the grassroots level. In many respects, it would make for more of an entertaining end product than what I had seen in over two decades following the Jets.

Following is a collection of the many off-the-wall stories along with an irreverent look at the characters behind them that make minor-league hockey unique.

Into the Abyss

The story of hockey's most unwanted team began with the tragic death of one of its most beloved teams.

In defiance of so many heroic last-ditch efforts to save the team, the Winnipeg Jets skated off the ice for the last time on Sunday, April 28, 1996. With their elimination in the first round of the Stanley Cup playoffs, the Jets' 24-season stay in Winnipeg was over. Though few in the city thought it was possible, hockey Armageddon had indeed come to Winnipeg.

The Jets began life as a charter member of the 12-team World Hockey Association (WHA) in 1972 and established themselves as the infant league's dominant team with three championships in seven years. They were not nearly as successful after joining the NHL in 1979, but they still remained a fixture in the community, beloved by all its citizens, even those who were not big hockey fans.

Over the years, the need to replace the decrepit Winnipeg Arena, the Jets' home rink, had become increasingly acute. The issue reached its climax in the 1990s as free agency in the NHL sent salaries skyrocketing. The Jets' owners were losing money hand over fist, and without a new facility, they were increasingly unable to keep pace in the new high-stakes NHL.

Unfortunately, the endless debates over who should fund this new arena became as divisive as any in the province's history. There were more interesting battles in boardrooms than on the ice as the three levels of government bickered among themselves and with the Jets' owners.

After the debates produced nothing but hot air, in the spring of 1995, the Jets announced they were leaving, most likely destined for Minneapolis. The news came as a dreadful shock to the people of

Winnipeg, a city of 700,000 on the eastern edge of the Canadian prairies that lived and breathed hockey. Jets fans felt immune to the rash of franchise relocations sweeping the continent. Many thought it just couldn't happen in Winnipeg. But it did.

Determined not to let their team leave without a fight, the people sprang into action. This was not just about a hockey team – it was a blow to their civic pride. The Jets were Winnipeg's only link to the big leagues and people felt that the loss of that link would relegate the city to backwater status.

That spring and summer, an emotional roller-coaster ride consumed the entire city.

Known nationwide for their frugality and thriftiness, Winnipeggers opened their wallets wide and raised over $13 million for an endowment fund that would be used to offset the club's losses and help fund a new arena. With a new ownership group entering the picture and the promise of some government funding, it looked like the team was going to stay after all.

As the summer dragged on, however, everything began to unravel.

The expected level of funding from the government was short. The new owners battled with the old owners over day-to-day control of the team. And in the end, there just wasn't enough money to pull it off, leaving the Jets to play one final season in Winnipeg before moving south, not to Minneapolis, but to Phoenix. All they would leave behind was a gaping hole in the heart of every Manitoba hockey fan.

Knowing the Jets were leaving, two rival ownership groups had purchased conditional interests in different IHL teams in late 1995 in order to keep pro hockey in Winnipeg. The Shindleman brothers had first purchased the Peoria Rivermen, and then a group led by Jeff

Thompson bought an interest in the Minnesota Moose. In a fateful decision that would profoundly and negatively affect Winnipeg hockey fans for decades to come, the IHL awarded Winnipeg relocation rights to the Thompson group.

The 'i' Generation is Coming.[2]

"For all intents and purposes, the Moose became a displaced team when the very real possibility surfaced that the Jets would move to the Twin Cities; that speculation has caused tremendous harm to the Moose. Therefore, ownership was given the right to relocate the franchise to a market where it has an opportunity to thrive," explained IHL commissioner Bob Ufer in the league's press release.

The IHL was founded on December 5, 1945, in Windsor, Ontario, in order "to provide opportunities for Detroit-Windsor hockey players returning home from World War II." It would prosper as a second-tier minor league in small towns around the Great Lakes region for decades until an aggressive expansion strategy promoted by Ufer saw them spread their wings across the continent.

Asserting itself as a top-tier minor league, the IHL had moved into major markets that didn't have or had lost NHL teams. As the Jets were winding up their final season in Winnipeg, the IHL had a total of 19 franchises scattered across North America between Los Angeles and Orlando.

I didn't know it at the time, but by expanding so aggressively, the league had effectively signed its own death warrant. Attendance and revenues skyrocketed, but so did expenses. Not only were travel costs much higher due to the geographic disparity between cities, but player costs would also rise substantially.

Angered by the IHL's move into major markets, the NHL gradually began transferring their affiliations to AHL clubs, where the focus was on development rather than selling tickets. As a result, IHL teams had to recruit and pay their own players. Years later, the IHL would again cozy up to the NHL, but unfortunately, far too late to be able to save the league.

The IHL had a surprising number of wealthy owners, but they were far less willing to accept significant financial losses than their NHL counterparts. For starters, an IHL team held virtually no resale value. Unlike the case in the NHL, owners could not fall back on the appreciating value of the franchise to justify losses on day-to-day operations.

Furthermore, little status or notoriety came with owning an IHL franchise. The NHL owner was often a revered, high-profile steward of a treasured community asset, whereas the IHL owner was an anonymous proprietor of a small mom-and-pop operation.

The Minnesota Moose became part of the league's aggressive expansion strategy when they were granted a franchise on December 20, 1993, shortly after the NHL's Minnesota North Stars had left for Dallas. Moose owners Kevin MacLean and Roger Sturgeon hoped to cash in by filling the void for hockey-starved Minnesotans. Instead, they would lose nearly $5 million over their two-year stay, languishing in virtual obscurity in the Twin Cities.

The Moose played out their second and final season in Minnesota as a lame duck following the announcement early in the year that the franchise was Winnipeg-bound. They went into a tailspin and their situation could best be described by an exchange between *Saint Paul Pioneer Press* beat writer Gary Olson and Moose player and former Jet Dave Christian in early March.[1]

"Do you want to make the playoffs?" asked Olson.

"It doesn't matter," replied Christian.

"Why?"

"Ownership. The team is leaving because it was neglected. These people thought, 'Oh, Minnesota doesn't have a hockey team so let's just put one there and we'll just make a lot of money.' As soon as the NHL says it might try to crack this market again, they use it as an excuse and leave."

The only thing going for the Moose was their highly marketable logo, which *The Hockey News* rated tops among minor-league teams. The Moose didn't sell many tickets or win many games, but they sold plenty of merchandise featuring the logo. In their last season in Minnesota, the Moose accounted for 20% of all league merchandise sales.

"This team logo is one of the most successful brand marks in the history of minor sports. Since its creation it has received numerous national awards, has appeared in several feature films and has generated millions of dollars in merchandise sales,"[2] stated the logo's original designer.

It was because of that logo that I was happy to learn of the IHL's decision to award relocation rights to the Moose ahead of Peoria. I developed an instant bond with the cute cartoon moose sporting a sly grin and holding a hockey stick with a forest scene in the background.

Before their arrival in Winnipeg, the Moose held a name-the-team contest, but the name "Moose" easily won out over Warriors, Cossacks, Minters, Snow Bears, Loons, Prairie Fire, Prairie Dogs, Sun Dogs, Ice Breakers, Blizzard, Terror and Skeeters. The name "Winnipeg Jets" was also on the ballot, and I was relieved that it didn't get many votes. This new team was not the Winnipeg Jets. For better or for worse, they needed to develop their own identity.

Unfortunately, few others would join me in becoming fans of the rechristened Manitoba Moose. Scorned and emotionally drained by the failed efforts to save the Jets, Winnipeg hockey fans were in no mood to warm up to the Winnipeg Arena's new anchor tenant. In addition, ownership would mimic the strategy the team had employed in Minnesota and just sit back and wait for hockey-starved fans to come charging through the doors. It was a fantasy that would never materialize.

Nonetheless, the lack of paying customers in the stands and interest around Winnipeg would not sway me from checking out what Moose hockey had to offer.

I jumped in with both feet to begin a colorful ride, one I would never forget.

1996-1997: The First Season

The Manitoba Moose officially began life on May 1, 1996, with an introductory press conference at the Arena, three days after the Jets had officially entered the history books.

Among the dignitaries in attendance was IHL commissioner Bob Ufer.

"I don't want to sound flippant but after the NHL hangover, I think people are going to be so relieved that the trauma and uncertainty is over that they can now embrace something and enjoy it and know that it's going to be there year in and year out."[1]

Winnipeggers could indeed embrace the Moose, but it is something they would never do.

At the press conference, the Moose announced that ticket prices would range from between $6 and $27. The IHL's agreement with the Professional Hockey Players' Association, which represented IHL players, had stipulated that a certain percentage of tickets in each IHL arena had to be priced under $10.

At the time, the Moose claimed they had 2,000 season ticket applications. I would later learn that any attendance or ticketing figure coming from the Moose organization would need to be independently verified before being accepted as true.

The next day, ominous storm clouds began forming over the relocated franchise.

Reports indicated a falling out between Jeff Thompson and partners Mark Chipman and original Minnesota owner Kevin MacLean. Thompson, the president of Woody Sports Apparel, had been the lead member of the group and had been front and center in the efforts to secure the Moose's relocation rights to Winnipeg. The resulting power struggle left him completely out of the picture.

"The Winnipeg Group of which I was an originating member started out the acquisition of an IHL team on the basis that all members would have an equal position and equal say in the partnership. The team was to have considerable local flavor and local influence. That was what I believed was the mandate and agreement of the Winnipeg Group. That is the basis upon which I started out and one of the key factors to me throughout. Approximately seven days ago, this basic understanding changed. After some discussion, I learned from Mark Chipman that he and Kevin MacLean have moved the original concept of the Winnipeg Group owning 50% of the team with local influence to one where the Winnipeg Group would be a minority interest holder and local influence would be considerably reduced. I opposed those changes and could not, in good conscience, accept them. Mark Chipman and Kevin MacLean decided to proceed without me and, as a result, I no longer have an active role as part of the current Manitoba Moose venture,"[2] said Thompson in a prepared statement.

The hole in the ownership group would later be filled by the Crocus Investment Fund, a labor-sponsored mutual fund. Crocus would acquire 24% of the club, leaving Chipman with 26% and MacLean with 50%. Eight years later, Crocus would stop trading and be eventually dissolved amid a scandal that spawned many accusations of impropriety. Years of litigation would follow.

Further reports indicated that Chipman would be making the decisions for the franchise. There would be no greater understatement in the annals of Winnipeg hockey history. He would soon become one of the most hands-on and high-profile owners in all of professional sports.

Mark Chipman.[7]

The CEO of Birchwood Automotive Group, Chipman had been a last-minute entry to what had been known informally as the "Thompson Group," which had once included former Jet Thomas Steen. Having retired as a player the previous year, Steen would have only a ceremonial role with the Moose. He was given the title of director of player development, but in August, he would leave for Germany, where he would resume his playing career.

Having succeeded in becoming the Moose's front man, Chipman immediately began searching for a coach. He spoke to former Jets coach Terry Simpson as well as former San Jose Sharks coach Kevin Constantine and former Jets player Paul MacLean.

Frank Serratore, the Moose's head coach and general manager for the past two seasons, clearly saw the writing on the wall. Though he was still under contract, he sought and received permission to interview for the head coaching position at the University of Nebraska–Omaha. After failing to land the post, he would return to the Moose and finish out the remaining year on his contract as the director of hockey operations.

In early July, Chipman gave former Montreal Canadiens and Quebec Nordiques coach Jean Perron a three-year deal to become the Moose's new head coach and general manager. The 49-year-old

Perron had been a last-minute entry into the coaching derby after Chipman had approached him at the recent IHL meetings in Winnipeg. Perron had been in attendance representing the dormant San Francisco Spiders franchise, with whom he was still technically employed.

I hated the Canadiens and didn't relish being on the same side as one of their former coaches, but I was pleasantly surprised that the Moose were able to attract someone of Perron's credentials. A Stanley Cup championship in 1986 highlighted his impressive resume. Last year, he had led the expansion Spiders to a successful season and home ice advantage in the first round of the playoffs.

I wouldn't be impressed for long. His postgame press conferences would prove to be more entertaining than his team's play.

"As long as you have the right leadership, you can build something stable and strong,"[3] said Perron.

Sadly, that leadership would be sorely lacking.

At the press conference announcing his appointment, a photographer had asked Perron to step to one side so he could snap a shot of Perron standing directly between the antlers in the Moose logo behind him. I was among many fans who were amused when the shot came out in the papers the next day, but Perron didn't quite see the humor in it.

"That was a stupid picture."[4]

That shot would come to define Perron's brief and almost comical tenure with the Moose.

Weeks later, the Moose named former Jets player and assistant coach Randy Carlyle as Perron's assistant. Carlyle had developed strong ties to Winnipeg ever since coming to the Jets via trade in 1984 and had preferred to remain in the city rather than follow the Jets to Phoenix or pursue another NHL job.

Not long after the announcement that the Minnesota Moose were moving to Winnipeg, I began to study the roster to see which players I might be seeing this year.

Their only star was former NHLer Stephane Morin, who had been the IHL's scoring leader a year earlier. Other notable names on the roster were former Jet Dave Christian, former WHA and NHL defenseman Gordie Roberts, former Penguins defenseman Jim Paek, former NHL player Chris Govedaris and tough guy Dave "Moose" Morissette.

I had never seen Govedaris play, but he had the catchiest surname of the bunch. I started picturing a scene of him leading a rush with the crowd chanting, "Go Go Govedaris."

Paek had won a Stanley Cup with the Penguins during an otherwise nondescript career, but he was a virtual celebrity to a good friend and former colleague of mine. Familiar with the Penguins on account of the fact that his wife hailed from Pittsburgh, he would constantly quote Penguins announcer Mike Lange's line of "Clear the track for Jimmy Paek."

The word "former" would come up frequently in any conversation about IHL players as most of them were either a former NHLer or AHLer. Since most of the league's teams were independent and had no NHL affiliation, they were left to find players for themselves. The only players that were available were aging veterans or one-time highly touted prospects who had not been able to stick on an NHL roster. Invariably, whenever I would be combing through an IHL roster, I would discover at least one long-forgotten name and ask myself, "Is he *still* playing?"

"The press guide is a collection of 'Where are they now?' stories,"[1] as one *Hockey Night in Canada* broadcaster would observe.

To my surprise, very few members of last year's squad would move north with the club, leaving the Moose to have to rebuild the roster almost from scratch. This would be a recurring theme, not just for the Moose, but for many teams around the league.

Most of the players in the IHL were on one-year contracts, leaving them free to pursue greener pastures elsewhere, either in the IHL or in Europe. Only the upper-echelon players could command a multiyear deal, and they were few and far between. It was the ultimate form of free agency.

There were no amateur drafts to prepare for, nor was there any need to develop prospects for the future. Aside from one or two players the odd club might keep on retainer in the lower minors, there was no farm system either. All the players that an IHL team had under contract were on the ice.

"The future is now," was a phrase coined by legendary Hall of Fame football coach George Allen. He would have loved the IHL.

As the Moose began signing players, I received a package from the team in the mail. Inside was a brochure and an awkwardly folded invoice for the same seat and same 14-game ticket package that I had for the Jets' final season. There was no letter of introduction, simply a message at the top of the invoice directing me to call their office if I had any "furthur" questions.

PLEASE FIND ENCLOSED YOUR MANITOBA
MOOSE INFORMATION BROCHURE. TO MAKE
YOUR PAYMENT OR IF YOU HAVE ANY FURTHUR
QUESTIONS CALL US, AT 987-PUCK

No, I had no "furthur" questions.[3]

It was a cold and impersonal first impression and a greeting more befitting the customer-hostile organization that had preceded them. I would later learn that Chipman had hired many of the people who had worked in the Jets' front office. It would prove to be the first among many mistakes Chipman would make and later repeat.

Over the course of my many dealings with the people in the Jets' front office, I had found each of them to be snotty, rude and apathetic. I was among many Winnipeggers who shed tears when the team left, but none of them were for the staffers in the front office.

I knew I wanted to see the Moose in action, but having never seen an IHL game before, I wanted to see some games firsthand before making any up-front commitment.

A couple of months later, I got a call from a Moose ticket representative. He told me that someone had wanted my seat as a season ticket, but as the existing ticket holder, I had the first right to upgrade from my mini-pack.

A likely story. That seat was 18 rows up in the corner behind the south-end goal. No one had wanted it for Jets games, and I knew no one would have wanted it now. It smelled of the same kind of high-pressure sales tactic I would have expected on a used car lot. Needless to say, I didn't fall for the hustle.

To humor myself, when I went to the box office to purchase my ticket for the home opener, I asked if that seat was indeed available. Not surprisingly, it was.

Meanwhile, the Moose slowly began assembling their roster for the coming season. They inked former Jets Randy Gilhen, Russ Romaniuk and Scott Arniel as well as 30-year-old former NHL goaltender Vincent Riendeau. The Moose also added Winnipeg native and former NHL player Carey Wilson, who was attempting a comeback after being forced to retire two years earlier because of knee problems. Regrettably, Wilson's knee problems would continue, and he would be forced to end his comeback less than a month into the season.

Other notables included Derek Nicolson, the son of the late Ken "Friar" Nicolson, the longtime voice of the Jets, and Teemu Numminen, the brother of Teppo, who had starred with the Jets for many years. Unfortunately, neither of them would make the team.

In addition to holdovers Morin, Paek, Morissette, Chris Jensen and Andy Schneider, the Moose rounded out their roster with a few veterans and youngsters hoping to make an impression.

1996-1997 Manitoba Moose Training Camp Roster

Goaltenders: Duane Derksen, Chris Gordon, Vincent Riendeau, Ed Skazyk

Defensemen: Kevin Barrett, Corey Beaulieu, Eric Brule, Chris Catellier, Gilbert Delorme, Jason Disher, Eric Dubois, Shawn Evans, Pat Hanley, Eric Lavigne, Derek Nicolson, Jim Paek, Martin Roy, Ken Sutton, Lindsay Vallis, Steve Wilson

Left Wingers: Scott Arniel, Dale Krentz, Kyle Millar, Keith Morris, Dave Morissette, Russ Romaniuk

Centermen: Dorian Anneck, Martin Bergeron, Randy Gilhen, Jeff Loder, Forbes McPherson, Stephane Morin, Teemu Numminen, Andy Schneider, Carey Wilson

Right Wingers: Shane Calder, Todd Holt, Chris Jensen, Claude Jutras, Darin Kimble, Scott McCrory, Craig Mittleholt, Greg Pankewicz, Darren Ritchie, Sean Tallaire

It was impossible for me to tell whether or not this was the makings of a good team or a bad team. Having suffered through endless years of mediocrity with the Jets, I kept my fingers crossed and hoped it would be the former rather than the latter.

Training camp began with medicals on September 14 followed by workouts at the suburban River Heights Community Center.

River Heights Community Center.[1]

"It's going to be a very, very tough week,"[5] vowed Perron.

One week later, I would be one of a couple of thousand visitors at the Moose's "Open Hoose" at the Arena. I watched the early workout and picked up a pair of foam antlers, one of the more popular souvenirs on sale. I've never worn them, but they remain an enduring symbol of a colorful era in Winnipeg hockey history and I refuse to part with them.

Those foam antlers would be one of the few Moose souvenirs I would ever buy. The tickets would definitely be more affordable, but the merchandise would not be. When the Moose's "Off the Rack" store later opened in front of the Arena, I was aghast when I looked at the price tags. Many items were not just as highly priced as their NHL equivalents, but often even more expensive.

Years later, a friend told me that she passed on buying a jersey for her young son because the jersey was priced higher than the combined cost of everything her son was wearing that day.

The outrageously priced merchandise would be one of many factors that would make the sighting of Moose paraphernalia in Winnipeg as rare as a sighting of Halley's Comet. The Moose logo was indeed popular, but right from the start, the organization had clearly overestimated its value. It would actually attain more of a following outside of Winnipeg than in its home city.

During the exhibition schedule, the Moose were less than impressive and seemingly had their minds elsewhere.

"Guys were out there retaliating and doing this and that. They didn't want to play hockey, they were just worried about the physical stuff,"[6] said Perron after the second of three straight losses to the Canadian national team, a squad made up of amateurs and semiprofessionals.

In the coming years, this touring national team would come to be an unofficial taxpayer-funded farm team for the Moose. All told, the national team would produce no fewer than 21 players for the Moose during their time in the IHL.

Though I didn't even know what role he played on the team at the time, I was shocked to learn that the Moose had traded Morissette. It seemed sacrilegious for the team to trade a player who carried the nickname of "Moose."

I would soon learn that Morissette had been the team's enforcer, a role that would have far more significance than I could have ever imagined. He had been replaced by Darin Kimble, who had signed days before the start of camp. Another former NHL player, Kimble was on his road back from a troubled past that included problems with alcohol.

As I would discover, there was a reason behind each player's banishment to the minor leagues. It could be off-ice problems such as Kimble's; injuries; lack of size, strength or speed; diminishing skills; a poor work ethic; or just a lack of dedication to the game. I would see players that would fall into each of these categories during my eight seasons following the Moose.

Ready or not, the Moose traveled to Milwaukee for their first league game against the Admirals at the Bradley Center on Friday, October 4.

Ticket stub from the first Manitoba Moose regular-season game.[4]

Bradley Center.[5]

Eager to learn more about my new favorite team, I tuned in to CJOB radio that evening and prepared to endure Kelly Moore's broadcast of the game. The voice of the Jets for the past two seasons, Moore would regrettably continue in the same capacity for the Moose.

Moore was well-spoken and well-prepared, but he would do little but fill the airwaves with the details of every skirmish and battle and lose focus on the game itself. At the final buzzer, I would know next to nothing about how the game went besides the final score.

Just as he had been with the Jets, Moore proved insufferable. I would listen to the postgame show on my way home only so I could catch some player interviews along with Perron's nightly tirade on how badly his team had played.

In between interviews, Moore would give who he thought the three stars should have been and represent them as "the three stars," as if his opinions were official. Not surprisingly, his opinions on who the stars should have been often varied greatly from mine and those announced in the building. I would often wonder if he had watched the same game I did.

Shockingly, Moore would win the IHL's broadcaster of the year award not once but twice. Those who voted for him must not have been fans who had tried to listen to his broadcasts.

Somehow, I managed to make it through the entire broadcast that night. The Moose seemed to be the better team, but the Admirals tied the score late in the third period, sending the game to the shootout.

For the past decade, rather than a more traditional overtime period, the IHL had used the controversial penalty-shot contest to decide tied games. Beginning with the visitors, each team would alternate shooters through five rounds or until a winner was decided. The winner would get two points in the standings, while the loser would receive one point. The shootout was reviled by hockey purists yet seemingly adored by casual fans for the entertainment value.

The issue was not decided until the Admirals' Larry DePalma scored in the final round to send the Moose down to defeat. A rugged winger and anything but a sniper, DePalma had scored only nine goals for the Moose last season in Minnesota.

This would be the first of many shootout losses to come for the Moose. Their lack of success in the shootout would become one of the franchise's defining characteristics throughout their years in the IHL.

Stopping them on this night was Admirals goaltender Danny Lorenz, who would come to dominate the Moose more than any other IHL goaltender, especially in the shootout. Using an aggressive style and timely, nimble poke checks, he would stop all but one of the 22 shots he would face in the shootout against the Moose this season. The minor-league journeyman would face the Moose a total of 13 times over the next two seasons and post a gaudy record of 9-3-1.

After a 5-3 loss in Las Vegas the following night, the Moose came back from an early 2-0 deficit on Sunday afternoon to beat the Long Beach Ice Dogs 5-3 for their first win of the season.

The Ice Dogs were playing their second game in their third home city in as many years. They had begun life as the San Diego Gulls six years earlier, but a sharp drop in attendance had prompted a move to Los Angeles. The team had drawn even fewer fans in Los Angeles, so they moved once again, this time to nearby Long Beach.

Although this would be an extreme case, frequent franchise movement would be an unfortunate fact of life in the minor leagues. As soon as the ledger began to show red ink, teams were either disbanded or packed up and moved.

This grueling ternion of weekend games would be the first of many for the Moose. Prime weekend dates were golden in the minor leagues, where the need to maximize every opportunity for a large crowd was paramount, unlike the NHL, where large crowds could be counted on any night of the week.

The need to force-feed as many weekend dates as possible would result in many strange scheduling anomalies. For example, the Moose would often play three games over a weekend, then have nearly an entire week off.

Further complicating scheduling issues was the fact that many IHL teams shared their respective arenas with National Basketball Association (NBA) teams. The NBA team would get priority on arena dates, leaving their IHL tenants to try to fit their schedule around the remaining available slots in the calendar.

"This is part of the IHL and a little bit of what's going on in professional sports, where it's controlled by Americans who don't know anything about hockey,"[7] said Perron.

Perron was not the only coach to decry IHL scheduling, but it was just another unfortunate fact of life in minor-league hockey. Coaches had to adjust by putting a greater emphasis on conditioning so that their teams could withstand the rigors of playing on three consecutive days, often in three different cities. In the NHL, scheduling games on back-to-back days is frowned upon and kept to a minimum.

After a loss in Utah to wrap up their season-opening road trip, the Moose flew back to Winnipeg to prepare for their home opener against the Las Vegas Thunder on Friday, October 11. Despite the game's historic significance, there was no guarantee of a sellout and I was able to procure a good seat an hour before the opening faceoff. All tickets were eventually sold, however, but it would be one of very few legitimate sellouts they would ever have.

The Arena's seating capacity was just over 15,000, but the Moose had made the decision not to open the upper decks during the season unless demand warranted. Seating capacity was thus reduced to just under 11,000.

Buoyed by the sellout crowd, the Moose would later take out an ad brazenly proclaiming that "hockey was alive and well in Manitoba, and the Moose aren't about to let up."[11] There was reason to be encouraged by the large turnout, but it was foolish to believe the Moose were going to become an instant success story because of one sellout crowd.

I said to myself at the time that the true measure of success for the Moose would be what kind of crowd they could draw on a cold, snowy Wednesday evening in the middle of January to see the Milwaukee Admirals. Within weeks, my theory would be put to the test. It would indeed prove to be a harbinger of the many years of apathy and indifference that would follow.

After taking my seat, my eyes were instantly drawn to the Moose's new uniforms, which were much different from what they had worn in Minnesota. The popular logo still adorned the front, but there was a thick, black angled stripe along the bottom accenting the white jersey with a pale, greenish-blue trim. It was a hideous design and the jerseys looked like cheap knockoffs of Disney's Mighty Ducks of Anaheim. With Disney's ownership of the Mickey Mouse character, I remembered when Wayne Gretzky once called the New Jersey Devils a Mickey Mouse organization many years earlier. That characterization would also accurately describe the Moose organization.

I also noticed the extensive renovations that had taken place in the north end, just a few rows below my vantage point. Though the work was still incomplete, the north-end ice-level seating area had been replaced by a club lounge, and new plush purple seats filled the north end. The $1.4-million renovation would also include a new souvenir store at the front entrance where a beer garden used to be.

It was sad to see that it took the Jets' departure to force Winnipeg Enterprises, the Arena's landlord, to make these badly needed renovations. The seating area had been in a state of disrepair for years and was undoubtedly one of the many sticking points in the contentious battles between the Jets and Enterprises. For all I knew, the Jets might not have left if the same concessions had been made for them.

As game time drew nearer, an air of curiosity filled the building. For the first time in a quarter-century, the Arena had a new anchor tenant. It was a new team in a new league and, like me, hockey fans wanted to see what lay in store. I scanned the lower bowl and recognized many familiar faces from my years attending Jets games, faces that would slowly begin disappearing over time.

The pregame show featured a magic show put on by a trio of energetic teenagers called the Mooseskateers. Their primary responsibilities were to set up the various intermission events and to sling T-shirts, hotdogs and beef jerky into the stands. Those sticks of ground-up scrota from assorted farm animals would prove strangely popular.

In these early years, they would use a giant slingshot, but they would later graduate to an air cannon. Strapped to one of their backs, the cannon could launch a hotdog from ice level all the way up to the upper deck.

Whatever the Mooseskateers would send into the stands, children would run after it like it was a gold brick. I remember one occasion when they fired a handful of cheese sticks in my direction and one of them landed in the hood of my parka. Before I could reach behind me and pluck it out, one of the children beat me to it. These freebies would prove to be one of the biggest attractions of the night for the kids.

The Mooseskateers load up the air cannon.[1]

Also making his debut in Winnipeg was Mick E. Moose, the team's mascot.

Mick E. Moose.[1]

Mick would become one of the most recognizable and popular figures associated with the team. Children would be drawn to him like flies, and only the Moose's fighter would attract more interest from the kids than Mick.

The Moose would later introduce Mick's twin brother, Mick Evil Moose, at one game. In his short-lived debut, Mick Evil spent the night stalking and beating up his more celebrated brother. The purpose of this stunt left much to the imagination, and mercifully, Mick Evil was never seen again.

After the Mooseskateers finished warming up the crowd, it was time for Winnipeg hockey fans to meet their new team. One by one, each member of the new and hopefully improved Moose skated out through a pair of inflatable antlers and took their places along the blue line while the fans politely applauded. Following the obligatory singing of the national anthems, the moment so many fans had been dreading for decades was at last at hand. It was time to drop the puck and officially begin the next era of hockey in Winnipeg.

Once the game got underway, the Moose put many of their new fans to sleep as they slogged through a dull, plodding 1-0 loss. In missing countless opportunities to dent the scoreboard, they served only to highlight their inept offensive attack. The only signs of life from the crowd came during each of the three fights that took place.

I left the Arena that night saying to myself, "Gee, there's a lot of fights in this league."

Fighting was indeed much more prevalent, and it would be a much more vital part of the game in the IHL. Seemingly more important than a top goal scorer, a heavyweight fighter was a must for each team. The loudest cheers of the night were reserved for the prearranged battle between these heavyweights and there was no less enthusiasm for the many undercard bouts between the respective middleweights. As the fights riled up fans and players alike, IHL games would sometimes take on the feel of an earlier era when Roman gladiators staged duels to the death in front of bloodthirsty crowds.

I never really enjoyed fighting at hockey games, but I would become fascinated by its critical importance in the IHL. It would be no accident that, throughout their time in the IHL, the Moose's heavyweight fighter would be among the team's most prominent and popular players.

Over the next five years, the Moose would become better known for fighting than for anything else they did on the ice. They would lead the league in fighting majors once and on three other occasions finish in the upper half of the league. More than half of the Moose's games would feature at least one fight, and they would rack up more fights than points in the standings while in the IHL. As a result, I would commonly refer to them as the "Fighting Moose."

The three fights in the home opener reminded me of a promotion the Jets used to run years earlier called the "Hat Trick Club." Fans who bought a special hat were entitled to a discount at the souvenir booths if a Jet recorded a hat trick – three or more goals in a game. The Moose could have offered a similar promotion if the team had three or more fights in a game. During their time in the IHL, the Moose would record nearly twice as many of these fighting hat tricks as goal-scoring hat tricks.

Following the game, I noticed a young woman leaning over the glass vigorously applauding the Thunder as they left the ice. I thought nothing of it until I discovered who she was a couple of days later after dialing up on my 28.8 baud modem to retrieve the latest messages from the IHL mailing list at plaidworks.com. This was in the early years of the Internet when such a modem was cutting-edge technology and made you the envy of everyone on your block.

I had subscribed to this list months earlier and found it to be an incredibly good resource for news. Even after the Moose had moved to Winnipeg, it would be hard enough to find news on the home team, let alone from around the league. Long after their arrival, the Moose were regularly bumped to the back of the sports pages in favor of curling and high school girls volleyball.

One of the list members would regularly post the satellite coordinates for televised IHL games so that those of us, like me, with a C-band satellite dish could tune in. It not only supplemented the meager quantity of televised Moose games but also allowed me to catch other games from around the league.

Among the small but passionate collection of posters on that list was Fiona Quick, a student at the University of Minnesota School of Journalism and Mass Communication. She began posting in late March and soon became one of the regulars. In addition to adding her two cents worth on IHL-related topics, she would talk about Minnesotans who were playing pro hockey and pontificate on the prospects of the return of an NHL team to the Twin Cities. She would become most known, however, for her obsessive infatuation with Parris Duffus.

Duffus was a 26-year-old minor-league goaltender who had played for the Minnesota Moose last season and was now with the Thunder. He could not seemingly make a move without Fiona posting a comment about her favorite player. Even in games when he would sit on the bench, Fiona would post an observation or two about his facial expression. If a journalist anywhere in North America dared to mispronounce his surname as "doo-fus" rather than "duff-us," Fiona was all over it and would post a scathing condemnation. At every turn, she would also take the opportunity to promote Duffus's case for a call-up as if NHL executives were reading her posts.

"What can I say, I love the guy,"[8] she would later say in a list posting. The day before the Moose's home opener, Fiona posted a message in which she stated she was coming to Winnipeg from the Twin Cities to see the game against Las Vegas on Friday. She gave the name of her hotel, said what she would be wearing and described herself as a "blonde Valerie Bertinelli type,"[8] encouraging list members to come and see her to put a face to an e-mail.

Much to Fiona's delight, it was indeed Duffus who stopped all 24 Moose shots he faced to earn the shutout that night. After the game, she was up on her feet cheering Duffus as if he were a returning war hero. If it wasn't for the boards and the high glass, she probably would have run out onto the ice, wrapped her arms around him and planted a big, wet, sloppy kiss right on his lips.

The NHL call-up she had been dreaming about finally happened next year when the Phoenix Coyotes summoned Duffus to replace one of their injured goaltenders. For the next couple of weeks, she began frantically scouring the Twin Cities looking for any sports bar that might be showing Coyotes games.

Fiona fumed as Duffus remained stapled to the end of the bench, but he finally saw his first taste of NHL action when he replaced Nikolai Khabibulin during a game against the Vancouver Canucks. Needless to say, she posted every detail of what would be his only NHL appearance. Duffus played the latter half of the contest, and Russ Courtnall scored on a breakaway to write his name into the history books as the only NHL shooter to ever beat him.

Fiona also had an infatuation with diminutive centerman Andy Schneider, whom she would call "Schnooky," but it would pale in comparison to her outspoken admiration for Duffus.

It was after reading these posts from Fiona that the somewhat offensive term "puck bunny" first entered my vernacular. These fanatic female admirers, or groupies, were, however, far more common in the AHL than in the IHL.

The AHL was mostly made up of younger players who had recently graduated from the junior ranks. They were in their early 20s, unattached and on their way to possible NHL stardom. On the other hand, the average IHL player was generally older, often a family man, and no longer had the allure of being a rising star. As a result, the

AHL was a much better breeding ground for these type of "fans," and they would come out of the woodwork in droves when the Moose joined the AHL in 2001.

During a first-period stoppage in the opener, the Moose held a "Sing for Your Supper" promotion. Two contestants were raised up on a platform and each had to sing a verse with the crowd's applause deciding the winner of a free meal from the sponsoring restaurant. Needless to say, this short-lived promotion did not spawn any future Grammy Award winner's career, but many of us in the stands enjoyed a laugh or two at the contestants' expense.

This would be just the first of many promotions that would only get more comical and later outrageous.

An intermission favorite became "turkey curling," and later the "chicken challenge." In each case, contestants would hurl frozen poultry carcasses down the ice like a curling rock. The contestant whose carcass came closest to the target at the opposite end would win a prize.

Other regular intermission events included human bowling and human pucks.

Human bowling.[1]

Human pucks.[1]

Sitting on a mini toboggan, a human bowling contestant was flung down the ice by a giant slingshot in an attempt to knock down as many pins as possible at the opposite end. In the human pucks game, three contestants dressed up in giant foam pucks and raced around the ice in their street shoes.

One particularly humorous promotion was an annual event called "Dash for Cash."

Dash for Cash.[1]

Three contestants were given 30 seconds to try to scoop up as many dollar coins off the ice as they could. They quickly realized it was no easy task as the coins quickly froze to the sticky, wet ice. Nonetheless, with a cash reward dangling like a carrot in front of their noses, they desperately flailed away trying to pry the coins loose from the ice. The exhausted contestants almost seemed relieved when the buzzer sounded to put an end to the game. For two of them, their efforts went for naught as only the one who had gathered the most was allowed to keep the money.

Most of these promotions were in good fun, but I remember one night after the human bowling competition when two of the Mooseskateers laid down on the ice between a pair of foam pins. To my horror, Mick E. Moose then began skating towards them as if he was going to try to make like Evel Knievel on skates and jump over them.

Mick goes airborne.[1]

Fortunately, Mick cleared them with ease, but I couldn't imagine why those poor Moosekateers would agree to such a thing. If anything had gone wrong in this ill-conceived stunt, Mick's skates could easily have sliced right through them and possibly killed them.

As all this frivolity was taking place on the ice, the radio-controlled blimp circled overhead during each intermission break.

Still adorned with the Minnesota Moose logo, the blimp made its debut on opening night and would be a fixture at every Moose home game. At first, it was just a nice little attraction, but it soon became a hazard after they began using it to drop coupons.

The blimp.[1]

On a couple of occasions I was nearly trampled by small but ferocious armies of children madly pursuing these falling coupons. I had no idea what these coupons were for and the children likely didn't know either. All that was important was that a freebie was up for grabs, and they were determined regardless of who or what was in their way.

Fortunately, at most of the games I would attend, I was close enough to the overhang of the upper deck where the blimp could not safely fly.

The Moose were certainly not alone among their IHL brethren in staging zany promotions. In Chicago, they had events such as tricycle slalom races and a tire rolling contest. The Wolves also joined the Michigan K-Wings in coloring the ice green on St. Patrick's Day.

Scantily clad cheerleaders were not uncommon around the league, and many years later, the Moose would get into the act with their "Ice Girls."

One of the "Ice Girls."[1]

Their official purpose was to clear snow from around the net and along the boards during stoppages in the play. In reality, they were there to provide eye candy for an audience made up mostly of young boys. Aside from a bare midriff, they were attired in spandex from head to toe that was stretched so tightly it looked almost vacuum sealed, leaving little to the imagination.

After laying an egg in their home opener, the Moose put on a much better show one night later as they defeated the Wolves 3-1 for their first victory at the Arena. In addition to the crowd of 8,476, the Hanson Brothers from *Slap Shot* made an appearance.

"They also represent the toughness, zaniness and showmanship that is the IHL's style,"[9] said Rob Gialloreto, the Moose's director of communications.

Truer words could not have been spoken.

Slap Shot was a classic movie about the Charlestown Chiefs, a ragtag, downtrodden minor-league hockey team based in a small Pennsylvania mill town. After the announcements of the mill's closure and that the team would be folding, the Chiefs turned to fighting and other off-the-wall tactics to reverse their sagging fortunes.

The strategy paid off as Charlestown was soon abuzz over the Chiefs. On the ice, the Hanson brothers "scared the bejesus out of everybody," as Paul Newman, who played the role of the Chiefs' player-coach, would say. Newman's character would also use other creative tactics to help his team win. In one famous scene, he got under the skin of an opposing goaltender by taunting him about his wife being a "dyke." The goaltender was subsequently ejected, and without a backup, the other team was easy pickings for the Chiefs.

I had seen the movie before, but I quickly dismissed it as a piece of unrealistic fiction. It wasn't until years after I had started following the Moose that I realized the movie was much closer to a documentary than a work of fiction. In the coming years, I would find so many similarities between scenes and characters in the movie to what I had seen with the Moose that it would seem as though the script writer had based the movie on the Moose.

It would be fitting, indeed, that in later years, the Moose would play scenes from the movie on the video screens prior to each game.

The game against Chicago was not the first appearance at the Arena for the Hansons. Professional hockey players in real life, they each had played against the Jets when they were in the WHA. I had seen Dave Hanson rip the hairpiece off Bobby Hull's head during a playoff game against the Birmingham Bulls in 1978.

In the movie, the Chiefs would have a booster club, as did the Minnesota Moose in real life. The Manitoba Moose, however, would never have one, due largely to the lack of boosters. Nor would Winnipeg, unlike Charlestown with the Chiefs, ever be abuzz over the Moose.

The Moose's record fell to 2-6-1 after a pair of embarrassing defeats over the weekend to the previously winless Quebec Rafales. Though their play was uninspiring, the Moose kept the crowd entertained in their frequent battles with the Roberge brothers, Quebec's pugilistic brother act reminiscent of the Hansons in *Slap Shot*.

In addition, Marc Rodgers of the Rafales was ejected during the Friday night contest after allegedly using a racial slur on one of the Moose players. Years later, Rodgers would suit up for the Moose.

These would be the first two of eight matchups between the clubs this season, a scheduling anomaly that was Chipman's idea. Despite the vast geographic disparity between the two cities, he was hoping to build off the same brief rivalry that had existed between the Jets and Nordiques two decades earlier in the WHA.

Rather than build a rivalry, however, it turned into a logistical nuisance for the Moose. Travel to Quebec involved a cross-continent flight to Montreal, followed by a two-and-a-half-hour bus ride. It was on that same stretch of highway that the bus carrying the Jets in November 1980 nearly crashed in the aftermath of a snowstorm.

Though, by his own admission, it wouldn't work, it would not be the last time Chipman would become personally involved in scheduling opponents he wanted on the docket. He did, however, succeed in generating animosity. The Moose would have more fights and penalties in games with the Rafales than against any other opponent during their five years in the IHL.

During postgame interviews, Randy Carlyle would regularly refer to the Quebec team as the "Rafaels." Though it was probably an unintentional mispronunciation, I often wondered if it was a subtle tribute to Rafael Belliard, the starting shortstop for baseball's Atlanta Braves at the time. The Rafales were in their first season in Quebec after having moved from Atlanta over the summer.

The Moose continued to lose and by the end of October, Perron was at his wits' end.

"I'm upset. I'm at the end. I can't stand it."[10]

He traded speedy defenseman Jim Paek for lumbering winger Mike Stevens and benched Morin, the team's only legitimate star, but the beat went on.

They had Chicago at their mercy on one Sunday night at the Arena, only to be done in by a rash of stupid penalties and the work of 33-year-old goaltender Wendell Young. It would be the first of 32 times they would face Young, more than any other goaltender during their time in the IHL.

Young was a short, balding veteran who had more stickers on his suitcase than a travel agent. Drafted in 1981 by the Vancouver Canucks, he would become the only man in hockey history to have won the Stanley Cup, Turner Cup, Calder Cup and Memorial Cup.

I noticed he always had a beaming smile on his face when he would take off his mask after a game at the Arena. No doubt, part of the reason for that smile was the 15-9-2 record he would post against the Moose during regular-season play as well as his 4-2 record in playoff competition.

After his playing career, he would go on to become an assistant coach and later, the general manager of the Wolves, who would retire jersey #1 in his honor.

The Admirals made their first appearance at the Arena in late October. Though it wasn't quite January yet, it was the first test of my theory as to the true measure of how well the Moose would be accepted by Winnipeg hockey fans.

A crowd of only 4,895 came through the turnstiles on that cold, snowy midweek evening to see the Moose drop a frustrating 5-4 decision as their record dropped to 3-8-2. Unfortunately, it would be the first of countless numbers of games in which the Arena would be less than half full.

I was among the small crowd that night, more to see the Admirals than to see the Moose. I had developed an early fondness for their cute logo featuring an ornery sailor on skates carrying his stick high as if poised to "carve out a man's eye with a flick of the wrist," to borrow a line from *Slap Shot*.

I had also developed a kinship with their long-suffering fan base. In his informative posts on the plaidworks.com mailing list, Joseph Houk, one of the Admirals' most dedicated supporters, detailed their legendary failures at playoff time, which mirrored those of the Jets.

Throughout my eight years following the Moose, I would make an effort to attend most of the games involving the Admirals.

Houk would also regularly post a detailed FAQ on the IHL and each of its teams that he had developed and maintained with loving care. With the league receiving such little coverage in the mainstream media and even locally in Winnipeg, it would be the single most authoritative source of information on the IHL I would ever find.

It is the work of fans like Joseph Houk that helped make my experience following the Moose and the IHL so much more rewarding. It is unfortunate that these noble efforts so often go unrecognized by fellow fans and by team owners.

After another loss to the Admirals, the Moose won for only the fourth time in their first 15 games when they spanked the lowly Phoenix Roadrunners by a score of 5-1.

With his team still in a downward spiral, a fuming Perron pulled the trigger on another major deal when he shipped Morin to Long Beach for marginal player Wayne Strachan.

"I had a discussion with Stephane on Tuesday morning and I realized at that time that this guy was not happy here,"[12] said Perron.

Perron would also later say that a contributing factor in the trade was that Morin had been complaining about the high taxes in Manitoba, a charge Morin would deny. So desperate were the Moose to rid themselves of Morin that they would even pick up a portion of his salary in Long Beach.

It is a trade the Moose would come to deeply regret.

I did not see enough of him to formulate an educated opinion, but having seen him so often in Minnesota, Fiona made him out to be a prima donna. In Long Beach, however, he would again become the same offensively dominant player he had been in Minnesota.

The trade appeared to be just the tonic the Moose needed as they swept a pair of games in Long Beach against Morin and the Ice Dogs. Randy Gilhen did a masterful job of checking Morin, and goaltender Fred Brathwaite chipped in with a goal of his own.

The Ice Dogs had pulled their goaltender during a delayed penalty call to the Moose, then made an errant backward pass that drifted the length of the ice and into their own net. As the last Moose player to touch the puck, Brathwaite was credited with the goal. It would be the first and only time in the league's 56-year history that a goaltender would be credited with a goal.

Though his goal was more of an accident, as he assumed the starting role, I would see for myself that Brathwaite was indeed a superior puckhandler. He had actually scored another goal four years earlier while playing junior hockey. Of the many goaltenders I had seen in person over the course of many years watching pro hockey, none could match Brathwaite's puckhandling prowess.

The Moose returned home and won their fourth in a row, only to drop a pair over the weekend to the K-Wings, the Dallas Stars' farm team. Since the Stars had become my favorite NHL team, I made sure to attend both games. I was still cheering for the Moose, but my eyes were more focused on the Stars' prospects.

Among them was goaltender Manny Fernandez. Though still thought to have a bright future, he'd been having mixed results in the Stars system over the past few years. He was outstanding in both games against the Moose, but as I saw more of him in future games at the Arena, I would come away unimpressed. In his brief appearances with the Stars, he would appear nervous and edgy and give the Stars little reason to keep him on the big-league roster. When the Stars later cleared the way for one of their goaltending prospects to make the team, he faltered and lost the competition to Marty Turco.

I was shocked when the expansion Minnesota Wild gave up a draft pick for him years later. Fernandez, however, would shine for the Wild. Had he played half as well when he was in the Stars system, he would not have spent so long in the minors.

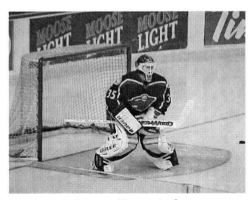

Manny Fernandez.[1]

Friday night's loss came in the shootout, and it was my first experience watching the penalty-shot contest firsthand. After the two-minute intermission following the end of regulation play, I moved up to the edge of my seat and watched former Jet Pat Elynuik take the puck at center ice and move in on Vincent Riendeau to get the shootout underway.

I was paying just as much attention to the crowd's reaction as I was to the confrontation on the ice. Like the entire experience with the Moose and the IHL, I approached the shootout with an open mind, but I had been hearing reports of how Winnipeg fans had hated it. The press reports turned out to be untrue as the fans rose to their feet and cheered wildly while all 10 shooters took their turn. The only louder cheers all night came in the second period when Darin Kimble took on Patrick Cote in a heavyweight fight.

With fighting so much more commonplace in the IHL, I would often wonder if it would not have been more appropriate to have a scrap between each team's enforcer decide the outcome rather than resorting to penalty shots. Such a "fightout" might have proved even more popular than the shootout. It is an idea the Moose may have been well advised to forward for consideration, since their failures in the shootout would become one of their enduring legacies.

No doubt, the shootout caused many sleepless nights for goaltenders around the league, but it was the referees who probably hated it more than anyone else. Already worn out from working a full game, the referee would have to skate the length of the ice between shots and position himself at the goal line as the opposing teams alternated shooters.

Despite the positive reviews the shootout received at the rink, Chipman and the Moose remained staunchly opposed to it. In a subsequent league vote, they were the only team to cast their ballot against it.

Then as now, I remain indifferent to the shootout. If fans enjoyed it, however, then I saw no reason to oppose it. My only issue with the format was that there was no true loser, since the losing team would still get a point in the standings. As a result, the extra points artificially inflated win-loss records, and even the teams at the bottom of the league could still technically boast a winning record. In fact, only four of the 19 teams in the IHL this season would finish with a sub-.500 record. To the uneducated observer, nearly every team in the league looked good.

The burst of energy the Moose received following the Morin trade proved to be short-lived, and they continued to struggle through November, remaining near the bottom of the league standings. To bolster their sagging fortunes, they scored a coup when they secured the loan of longtime NHL veteran Neal Broten from the New Jersey Devils. Sadly, hours before what would have been his first game with the Moose, the Devils found another NHL home for him when they traded him to the Los Angeles Kings.

To make matters worse, Ken Sutton, the Moose's best defenseman, was recalled by the St. Louis Blues, then later traded to New Jersey. Unaware that Perron had secured Sutton's minor-league rights from the Blues, the Devils assigned him to their AHL affiliate in Albany, touching off a sordid affair that would consume Perron's and Carlyle's attention for much of the season.

The two would hound the Blues for a replacement and St. Louis eventually agreed to send NHL veteran Gary Leeman to the Moose. Leeman, however, refused to report and would instead finish the season with the Utah Grizzlies. Following the Leeman affair, the Moose reluctantly gave up the fight.

Though the Moose were floundering and I figured they wouldn't last very long in Winnipeg, my interest in the team continued to grow. I found the level of play to be good and the ticket prices were much more affordable. There was a morgue-like atmosphere at the games, but I didn't need 15,000 energized fans around me to have a good time. I actually developed an appreciation for having half a section to myself.

It was this increasing interest that led me to develop a Web site devoted to the Moose that went live at the end of October. In the years to come, I would make my first foray into writing when I began penning a column on the site called "View from Section 26," named for the section where I could be found on most game nights. At the time, the quality of my writing was very poor, but it has developed and become so much more than what started out as a hobby. It is something I have enjoyed immensely and likely would not have pursued were it not for my interest in the Moose.

In later years, I would regularly take a notepad with me and take notes during games. Other fans would sometimes ask if I was a reporter, since the sight of someone in the stands who actually appeared to care about the proceedings was so rare that it would naturally draw attention.

Interestingly, that column would land me a short-lived presence at the fledgling site HockeyInsiders.com. With the backing of a former editor of *The Hockey News*, they had hoped to become a comprehensive source for news on major and minor pro teams as well those from the junior ranks. That site never got off the ground, however, and it was just as well as far as I was concerned. I had written about the Moose because I wanted to, not because I had to. I wanted to be there as a fan, not as a paid staffer. It bothered me that it had become a job, and it made the games less enjoyable during my brief period as their Moose beat writer.

As I look back, I should have suspected that hockeyinsiders.com would never amount to anything. Since the columnists were anything but Pulitzer Prize candidates, they must have been incredibly desperate for contributors.

That early site was amateurish in every respect, even for its day, when the Web was in its infancy. Though my database skills were strong, I was and remain a weak graphic designer. However, for the bulk of the time that I had followed the Moose, my site was far more informative than the team's official site. I would offer rosters, schedules, game reports and player profiles, none of which the Moose would feature on their own site.

The fact that they were being humiliated online by a fan's part-time hobby was evidently of no concern to the Moose. It would be several years before the club would care enough to develop anything resembling a useful site of their own.

On account of the Moose's weak online presence, despite prominent notices to the contrary, many visitors would confuse my site with the team's official site. That confusion would be an ongoing source of annoyance for both me and the Moose.

On one occasion, two would-be hopefuls sent me resumes in the hopes of getting a tryout with the Moose. Out of courtesy, I forwarded them on to Rob Gialloreto, who candidly admitted they had received many such resumes from players who underestimated the quality of play in the IHL.

"They don't realize how good this league is until they get here," said Gialloreto in an e-mail response to me.

What became a far greater nuisance to me was the flood of e-mails I would get from people outside of Winnipeg asking me to buy items such as game programs and jerseys for them. Naturally, the Moose had no online store of their own, so any fans looking for souvenirs featuring the popular Moose logo had little other choice than to take their chances with me.

Had I been more of an enterprising entrepreneur, I could have made some extra money as a reseller of Moose merchandise. However, this was in an era where online payments and e-commerce in general, much like the Web itself, were very much in their infancy and the extra bother just wasn't worth it to me.

Increasingly fed up with these e-mails, I would eventually create a Frequently Asked Questions section on my site in which the first item stated that I wasn't a reseller of Moose merchandise.

For their part, Chipman and the Moose would have no cause to complain about the confusion between the two sites. Rather than working to develop their own site, they would elect to spend more of their time and effort monitoring mine. They were not at all appreciative of my patronage and efforts to promote the team and they would only respond with snarky retorts to my commentary.

I would find Chipman, in particular, to be extraordinarily thin-skinned and hypersensitive to criticism, taking each and every negative word as a scathing personal insult. Instead of turning his attention in-house and taking constructive steps to address the issues of customers like me, he would later opt to hire a lawyer and threaten me with legal action.

I laughed years later when I recalled that Rob Gialloreto, before leaving the Moose, told me, "Your site is the ultimate tribute to our organization."[35]

My interest in the team and running my Web site would also lead me to the purchase of my first camera. Over a four-year span, I would snap more than 2,000 pictures at games and other Moose events, and I would put some of the best shots on my site. I would eventually become such a shutterbug that I would wear out a camera after taking more than 38,000 pictures with it over the span of three and a half years.

There would be many odd scheduling quirks during the Moose's history, but perhaps none stranger than the three-game set that appeared on their schedule in early December. On a Wednesday night, they would entertain the Orlando Solar Bears, then fly to Milwaukee to meet the Admirals on Thursday before returning home for a rematch with Orlando on Friday. While their opponents were in Milwaukee, the Solar Bears would remain in Winnipeg for a day of rest.

In Wednesday's opener, the red-hot Solar Bears cruised to an easy 7-3 victory. The biggest story of the night was the work of referee Conrad Hache, whose controversial calls late in the second gave Orlando a series of power-play opportunities. The visitors took full advantage by scoring three times to break the game wide open. As simmering tempers reached a boiling point, Hache completely lost control and the game turned into a slugfest. No fewer than five fights broke out in the third, and even the two coaches got into a shouting match between the benches.

Before the season, Perron stated, "You have never seen anything like the officiating in this league."[13]

His words would indeed prove prophetic as this would be the first of many bad experiences the Moose would have with IHL officials. However, like the players themselves, the officials were also not of major-league caliber, as Perron had acknowledged during the exhibition season.

"We don't get the best referees in the world in the IHL. We get the second-best guys that the NHL are grooming so they're bound to have many bad nights. We have to be prepared for that."[14]

Unfortunately, Perron would often disregard his own advice and the Moose would suffer accordingly. So often, as on this night, they would lose their composure after a series of questionable calls and take themselves completely out of the game. Sadly, this would be a recurring theme that would continue long after Perron's dismissal.

In later years, the officiating would only get worse as the IHL would switch from using developing NHL referees to their own in-house candidates. These new referees, often former linesmen, were part-timers who were paid a paltry $225 per game. On one occasion after a Sunday afternoon game in Winnipeg, the referee immediately flew back to his home in Windsor, Ontario, in time to take his night shift at the Chrysler plant.

The linesmen would, for the most part, escape the limelight during my time following the Moose. I hadn't paid much attention to them until I began noticing the same names being announced before each game. I would later learn that the IHL assigned linesmen from a pool in each respective city. In Winnipeg, there would be a rotation of three or four who worked minor hockey games throughout the city.

Like the referees, the linesmen were also part-timers. One of them was Ryan Galloway, who was a third-year university student when he first began working Moose games. From these humble beginnings, he would emerge as a rising star and eventually go on to work as a linesman in the NHL.

After losing in the shootout for the third time in as many visits to Milwaukee, the Moose returned to Winnipeg and spanked the rested Solar Bears 6-3 for their first win in six outings. I was among 7,837 paying customers who received a candy cane smaller than my pinky finger on my way through the front doors.

Not long after taking my seat, my jaw nearly hit the ground when I saw none other than Mark Chipman bounding up the steps in full gallop in the aisle to my right. During the hundreds of Jets games I had attended over the years, I never once spotted owner Barry Shenkarow at a game. The sight of Chipman in such close proximity was yet another in a series of indicators that told me Moose hockey was going to be a very different experience from anything I had seen with the Jets.

Leading the Moose on Friday night was Greg Pankewicz, who was named the game's first star. The team's second-leading scorer, Pankewicz had signed with the Moose over the off-season after spending the latter half of this past season in Chicago.

Despite his short stay with the Wolves, Pankewicz quickly developed a reputation for his temper. Regrettably, it is that temper that would also define his tenure with the Moose.

Though prone to long dry spells, Pankewicz would score a team-leading 74 goals over the next two seasons. He would also lead them in temper tantrums, lashing out at officials and/or opposing players, often at critical moments late in games, resulting in innumerable penalties that would crush the Moose's chances on many nights.

Pankewicz's explosive temper had few equals at any level of organized hockey.

Interestingly, he would keep a gargoyle above his stall in the locker room at the Arena, a gift from his wife "to keep away the demons."[16] A case of gargoyles could not keep away the demons from the mercurial Pankewicz.

"Getting the most out of Pankewicz could be the stuff of a sports psychology study," said Ashley Prest of the *Winnipeg Free Press*. "Some games, he is the most dominant player on the ice. Other nights, he fades in and out. On still other nights, he's like a time-bomb ticking before ending up in the penalty box."[15]

It was Pankewicz's fiery intensity that drove him to become a dominant offensive force in the IHL. It would be his inability to harness that intensity and channel it in a positive way that kept him not only from being more of an asset to the Moose but also from advancing up the ranks to the NHL.

His temper would remain a hallmark characteristic even after his playing career. While serving as an assistant coach with the Colorado Eagles, upset over an official's call, he stripped half naked as part of yet another tirade before finally leaving the bench.

Though Pankewicz was an extreme case, despite the slower pace of the games, there was just as much, if not more intensity in the IHL than there was in the NHL. Unlike the NHL, players were not celebrities with rock-star status. They were common, everyday working people battling for meal money and to put food on their tables, not just for bragging rights on the next day's sportscast. I could plainly see that determination written all over their weary, battle-scarred faces even from my vantage point in the upper reaches of the Arena.

The Moose continued to stagger along as they had only a 5-4 shootout win in Quebec to show for a four-game road swing. The low point of the trip was an 8-1 blowout loss to the Detroit Vipers that was seen by a national television audience across Canada.

"It's the worst game of the season, a total embarrassment to the organization,"[17] said Perron after the game in Detroit.

A week before Christmas, badly in need of a goal scorer, Perron made another move when he sent Chris Jensen to Quebec for 33-year-old journeyman Chris Kontos. In his first game with the Moose, Kontos was hit in the face with the puck and had to leave the game with a bloody gash and a concussion. Despite the inauspicious debut, however, he would miss only one game and go on to enjoy a fine season for the Moose. Jensen, meanwhile, one of the team's last remaining ties to Minnesota, would opt to retire rather than report to the Rafales.

Following another pair of defeats, Perron's next move was to send Mike Stevens to the Cincinnati Cyclones for veteran defenseman Dale DeGray. Oddly, it was the second time the two players had been traded for each other. Two years earlier, the Cleveland Lumberjacks had traded DeGray to Cincinnati for Stevens.

Backed by Fred Brathwaite's goaltending, the Moose responded by taking all three games of a home stand between Christmas and New Year's. The diminutive Brathwaite had taken over the starter's role from an ineffective Vincent Riendeau and would carry the load in goal for the rest of the season. Riendeau would become such a fixture in the backup goaltender's chair next to the bench that I would come to refer to it as "Chateau Riendeau" long after he had left the Moose.

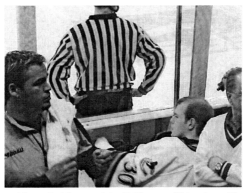

Alex Auld seated in "Chateau Riendeau."[1]

Brathwaite would become one of my favorite players. He had a pleasant, easygoing demeanor and always had a beaming smile that shone brightly throughout the Arena.

I fondly remember his routine when he would lead the Moose out to start the game. While his teammates raced past him, he would slowly hug the red line until reaching the opposite side of the ice. He would then tap his stick on the top of the boards and take off like a shot towards the goal.

In sharp contrast to many athletes today, he was also one to always selflessly give the credit to his teammates after a good outing rather than accept any praise for himself.

It would come as quite a surprise when the Moose cast him adrift following two solid seasons. Little could he have imagined, however, that it would be the biggest break in his career.

After catching on with the Canadian national team, Brathwaite signed with the Calgary Flames, where he soon moved into the starting role and held it for three seasons. He would go on to play two years with the St. Louis Blues, and he made his last NHL appearance for the Columbus Blue Jackets in the 2003-2004 season.

The Moose would frequently run into goaltending problems in the coming years and each time, I would remember the mistake they had made in letting him go.

Riding a modest three-game winning streak, the Moose hit the road for three games over the weekend.

"I think we've turned the corner,"[18] boasted Perron.

Around that corner would be a blind alley.

The Moose looked awful in dropping the first two games in Long Beach, and only Brathwaite's heroics enabled them to salvage a win in Houston on Sunday afternoon. After splitting a pair of games at home, the Moose hit the halfway mark sporting the second-worst record in the 19-team league.

"Just give us some time. This is professional hockey, not midget, but we're a first-year operation with a very strict budget and the owners do not want a repeat of last year in Minnesota where they lost about $3 million,"[19] said Perron.

Perron didn't have time. His team was floundering and he undoubtedly saw the writing on the wall. Despite the public plea for patience, he would be fired three weeks later.

Making his debut during the brief home stand was 20-year-old Russian Alexander Korolyuk, a sixth-round pick of the San Jose Sharks. Unable to sign with the Sharks this year due to a technicality, Korolyuk accepted the Moose's offer rather than report to the Sharks' AHL affiliate.

He would do little to counter his advance billing as a "chippy, attitude-prone competitor,"[20] but he would give the Moose some badly needed offensive punch. Unfortunately, it would come far too late to save their season.

Getting settled in Winnipeg would prove problematic for Korolyuk on account of the fact that he spoke no English. As someone who had spent last season in Germany without speaking German, Riendeau understood the difficulties Korolyuk was facing and opened his home to the youngster to help with the transition. Though he would do little besides warm the bench for the rest of the season, by helping Korolyuk, Riendeau would still make a positive contribution to the team.

Another pair of defeats on the road in Quebec and Chicago put the Moose five points back of a playoff berth.

In the 5-3 loss at the Rosemont Horizon in Chicago, scoring twice and adding one assist was Steve Maltais, the Wolves' top scorer.

Steve Maltais.[1]

In the coming years, he would become known as a Moose killer. His total of 35 regular-season goals along with six more in the playoffs would be far more than any other player would score against the Moose during their time in the IHL.

Maltais didn't just save his best work for the Moose, however. He would become a four-time 50-goal scorer and be as dominant an offensive force in the IHL as Wayne Gretzky or Mario Lemieux in the NHL.

It surprised me that there were any long-tenured, star-quality players in the IHL. I had thought that as soon as a minor-league player showed any promise, an NHL team would promote him right away. Maltais would indeed get his chances, but he would never be able to stick on an NHL roster. Each time an NHL opportunity came and went, after returning to Chicago, he would pick up right where he left off and continue lighting up scoreboards across the IHL.

From a distance, he looked like anything but a star hockey player. He could easily have passed as the guy who picks the garbage up off my curb or a construction worker on the side of a highway. A hard hat would probably fit him better than a hockey helmet.

It would be another sign of how IHL players were simply regular working stiffs just trying to earn a living, much like the fans who came to see them play. It was an endearing quality that would make me appreciate the IHL much more over the coming years.

After 11 spectacular seasons in Chicago, the Wolves would retire jersey #11 in his honor.

Steve Maltais' #11.[6]

Despite a dazzling outing from Korolyuk, the Moose blew a two-goal third-period lead in a sloppy defensive effort against Las Vegas and lost their fourth straight. The Moose played without defenseman Martin Roy, who had abruptly quit the team earlier in the day. He would later blame captain Randy Gilhen, claiming, in an interview with *Le Journal de Quebec*, that Gilhen "was always on my back."[21]

That night, in a pregame ceremony, Mark Chipman presented legendary Winnipeg sports fan Gabe Langlois, more commonly known as "Dancing Gabe," with a special #1 jersey and a season ticket for life.

Over the past decade, Gabe had become something of a local celebrity. He attracted attention when he began dancing in the aisles during breaks in Jets games as well as Blue Bomber football games and Goldeyes baseball games. During the much-publicized fight to save the Jets in 1995, Gabe even got some air time on news superstation CNN.

Dancing Gabe.[1]

Unfazed by the Jets' departure, he continued his tradition at Moose games while wearing a jersey modeled after the style the team wore in Minnesota. He would, however, soon switch to the new jersey that Chipman had presented to him.

Gabe grew up as a special-needs child and didn't speak until he was 10. Despite living with a condition that his mother describes as autism, he is never without a smile on his face and he has always maintained a positive outlook.

Gabe would not be the only member of his family to be prominently featured at Moose games. His brother, Mike, would later work as a linesman and a referee in the IHL and would frequently be on the ice while Gabe was performing in the stands.

When I was at Canada's Sports Hall of Fame in Calgary in June 2013 signing copies of my first book, someone from Winnipeg approached me and said I was as famous as Gabe. I took that as a compliment.

The Moose won only one of the first four games of a five-game road trip to fall 10 points back of a playoff position.

"We made stupid, stupid mistakes. We make life so easy for other clubs, it seems like they're walking [in alone] on our goalie all the time,"[22] said Perron after another loss in Quebec to close out the month of January.

Before leaving on the trip, the Moose surprisingly waived Darin Kimble, their leading fighter. Though many of his teammates had been struggling, Kimble established himself as the league's premier pugilist. He had become so feared, in fact, that no one else wanted to fight him, making him useless to the Moose. In effect, he had fought his way out of a job.

Oddly, though no one wanted to fight him while he was with the Moose, his eventual replacements were more than willing to drop the gloves with him after he had been picked up by Kansas City.

The Moose wrapped up the trip with a visit to Kalamazoo to battle the K-Wings at Wings Stadium.

Wings Stadium.[5]

Wings Stadium was a quaint little rink with a capacity of just over 5,000 that had served as the team's home for more than two decades. Though small in size, it had plenty of charm and character and was more than adequate for an era in which the IHL was a lower-tier league with its cities concentrated within a short bus ride of each other.

Kalamazoo and Fort Wayne were the last two holdovers from that era. In many respects, they had become like the Green Bay Packers of the National Football League. The Packers were founded in a similar era when the league's teams were in smaller urban centers separated by no more than a day's bus or train ride.

The Packers were the only one of those so-called "town teams" to survive the league's move into major markets, but Kalamazoo and Fort Wayne would not be so lucky. Lower-tier leagues, however, would see the wisdom in taking in both cities.

Playing their fourth game in five nights, the Moose put up a tough battle, but they still dropped a hard-fought 1-0 decision to the K-Wings.

"We have to do something, there's no question,"[23] said an exasperated Perron.

The Moose did do something. The following evening, Chipman fired Perron.

"I had hoped to see more positive energy develop in the last week after we had talked about it more than a week ago," said Chipman, who had taken in the last two games of the road trip. "It was a style and an approach that wasn't working with the players and team we'd assembled."[24]

As the losses continued to pile up, a desperate Perron had resorted to ranting and raving to inspire his charges. His tactics backfired badly. Players had grown increasingly resentful of Perron's stinging public criticism, and morale had sunk faster than the Moose's descent in the league standings.

A decade earlier in Montreal, Perron's thorny relations with his players had been no less problematic.

"Perhaps the best way to describe the Jean Perron era with the Montreal Canadiens is to say that he was a coach that I could never really get a handle on. It was probably less his fault and more mine, but here was a man who was my coach for three years and I never felt I knew him. It was not for lack of communication, we spoke on several occasions, most of them friendly, but something just didn't click," said Hall of Fame defenseman Larry Robinson. "He was a poor motivator and the team was almost ready to mutiny."[25]

In his defense, however, on account of being hired so late in the off-season, Perron was left with little chance to succeed in his first year on the job.

At the time, I felt his dismissal was premature. There were extenuating circumstances, and despite how badly he had handled the team, given his track record, he had earned more of an opportunity to prove his worth.

I had also come to enjoy Perron's postgame tirades, which were often more entertaining than the games themselves. Eschewing the tact and political correctness that has become so commonplace among media-savvy players and coaches, Perron would hold little back in blasting his team's most recent poor performance.

Though he was no longer on the payroll, Perron was far from finished with the Moose. Before leaving town, he called a press conference in which he laid much of the blame for his dismissal at the feet of captain Randy Gilhen.[26]

"I could see right from the start that Gilhen and Perron didn't click, connect very well," said Perron.

Perron also blamed Gilhen for the ill-advised trade of Stephane Morin earlier in the year.

"There was a personality conflict between Gilhen and Morin."

"But I'm going to take that responsibility. I was the GM and I should have known those facts a long time ago. Today I feel pretty bad about this. I don't think Stephane Morin deserved that kind of treatment. Later on, I'll apologize to Stephane Morin. We agreed to that trade. But it was not a very good trade."

Gilhen, naturally, was taken aback by Perron's comments.

"I'm really surprised and disappointed by that. In no way did I ever lead any mutiny. I'm as shocked as anybody he'd say that. ... There was never any problem between myself and Stephane Morin."

Perron didn't just stop with Gilhen. He went on to say that the "strong suggestions" that he hire Randy Carlyle and keep Frank Serratore also played a factor in the train wreck that the season had thus far become.

"I was kind of an outsider in this organization. I don't think we had the good chemistry between the three of us."

Perron would be the last outsider Chipman would hire. His future hires would come only from those who were already working for him or known to him through his cronies.

Three years after airing his dirty laundry, Perron would file a lawsuit against the Moose for wrongful dismissal. He also claimed the Moose had failed to pay him the $140,000 he had been owed on the final year of his contract and that he "suffered, and continues to suffer, damages with respect to loss of income and loss of reputation."[27]

In many respects, it would be fitting that the litigation would last a year and a half longer than the length of Perron's original contract.[28]

Perron's brief tenure behind the Moose bench would be his last job in the pros. He would go on to coach in Israel, giving a boost to their fledgling national program.

Chipman immediately named Carlyle as Perron's successor on an interim basis and vowed to reevaluate the entire hockey department after the season.

Randy Carlyle.[8]

Despite the new title, Carlyle would effectively function as Chipman's assistant instead of Perron's.

Over the coming years, both Chipman and Carlyle would repeatedly and interchangeably be quoted in articles discussing hockey matters. I heard radio interviews with Chipman in which he would speak of issues such as chemistry in the dressing room and what he felt needed to be changed. He sounded every bit like the general manager and I suspect it was a role he at least shared with Carlyle.

Even at this early stage, having only a dozen games under my belt as a fan, I began to notice that Chipman was quickly becoming the face of the franchise. As columnist Dave Jacober wrote on fanhub.me, "If your team's owner is more recognizable than the players or head coaches, then your team is dysfunctional."[29]

I couldn't have said it any better myself. I had always found that team owners were like offensive linemen in football – the less you heard about them, the better they were. Unfortunately for me and many other Winnipeg hockey fans, Chipman would fully validate my theory.

Carlyle had been an assistant coach with the Jets for the past couple of seasons, but he was best known to local fans from his playing days as a defenseman for the Jets. He had spent over a decade in a Jets uniform, during which he had established himself as one of the franchise's best and most well-respected players.

He had originally broken into the NHL with the Toronto Maple Leafs, but his career later blossomed with the Pittsburgh Penguins, where he won the Norris Trophy as the league's best defenseman. It is likely that no player in the history of the game ever got more mileage out of a Norris Trophy than Randy Carlyle. Each time Carlyle's name would be mentioned on radio or television, it would almost always be preceded by "former Norris Trophy-winning defenseman."

I would mouth the words "yes, we know" while seething after hearing of his Norris Trophy-winning season for the umpteenth time. Carlyle certainly had an outstanding playing career. However, many local media outlets had tried to make it appear as though Carlyle had been the greatest defenseman of all time.

Despite all of his success on the ice, he might be best remembered for one particularly embarrassing incident that took place in

December 1985 at the Arena. The last man back for the Jets, Carlyle was carrying the puck up the ice. Trailing the play, Bernie Nicholls of the Los Angeles Kings yelled, "Hey, Kitty," and Carlyle responded to the call of his nickname by blindly feeding a perfect pass onto Nicholls' stick. From my seat in the upper deck, I had a bird's-eye view as Nicholls went in alone and beat goaltender Daniel Bouchard.

To make matters worse, in a desperate attempt to get back in the play, Carlyle had fallen to the ice, injuring his thigh, causing him to miss the next four games.

"I guess my philosophy is pretty simple. I try to be as honest and straightforward with these guys as I can. And I don't dwell on the negative. I try to point to a player's strengths, not his weaknesses,"[31] said Carlyle on his coaching style, which would differ greatly from the approach employed by Perron.

His tenure would prove to be more successful than that of his predecessor, but his postgame press conferences would not be nearly as entertaining as Perron's were. In front of the microphones, he was stiff as a board, and unlike Perron, he composed his words with caution before opening his mouth. Time and again, he would do little else but trot out one or more canned lines from his small repertoire that he would recycle with clockwork precision.

"We received the level of goaltending required to win the hockey game," was his standard response when asked about his goaltender on any given night. It would come to be his most favored line to use after a game when speaking with reporters.

In his public appearances, Carlyle would carry himself like a rock star, unlike most IHL players and coaches who better fit the mold of a blue-collar factory worker. It was obvious that he enjoyed being famous, and he lit up like a Christmas tree when adoring children would swarm around him.

From his many years as a player with the Jets, he was indeed popular and a revered local celebrity. As a former Jets season ticket holder, I had come to appreciate his abilities as a player better than most. He would develop into a good coach, but his performance would be nothing out of the ordinary. It would be only Chipman's unshakable loyalty that would keep Carlyle behind the Moose bench for the next four years.

Once it became clear that Carlyle was hockey's equivalent of a teacher's pet, I would frequently refer to him as "Captain Crony."

The Randy Carlyle era began with yet another shootout loss, but the Moose followed with nine wins in their next 10 games. Alexander Korolyuk played like a man possessed as he toyed with his helpless opponents. Starting nearly every night, Fred Brathwaite was simply spectacular. In addition to picking up an IHL Goaltender of the Week award, he nearly scored another goal, but was foiled by a defenseman trailing the play.

"There was just a lot of tension in the room when Jean was coaching," said Scott McCrory, the team's leading scorer. "I think it's a lot more positive with Randy and I think we've responded."[30]

Fans began to notice and attendance picked up. Only four points back of a playoff spot, it looked as though the Moose were going to be able to pull themselves out of the massive hole they had dug for themselves.

Then cracks began developing in this papier-mâché foundation.

Chris Kontos pulled a groin muscle and missed time. Scott Arniel would be out for six games with a broken hand. Russ Romaniuk contracted mononucleosis, putting an end to his injury-plagued season. Playing more often than at any point in his pro career, Brathwaite began to show signs of wear.

The Moose remained in contention, but they began to fade in mid-March. Nine points in arrears of the last playoff position, the Moose began a critical four-game western road swing with a game in Las Vegas.

During their time in the IHL, the Moose would play in a variety of rinks, some big, some small, some new, some old. None, however, would be less suited for hockey than the Thomas & Mack Center in Las Vegas, a facility designed for basketball, with its court much smaller than a hockey rink. As a result, the Thunder were forced to play on a 180-foot rink, 20 feet shorter than a regulation-size surface.

In one end, many seats still had to be folded up to accommodate the shortened rink. The sight lines in this end were so bad that only fans in the first row could see inside the blue line. The rest of the fans in that end could see only the part of the ice from the near blue line on out.

Taking advantage of some weak goaltending from Parris Duffus, the Moose beat the Thunder 6-3 to keep those flickering playoff hopes alive. The Moose's cause was also bolstered by a pair of power-play goals they scored during a charging major assessed to Sasha Lakovic, who had taken a run at Brathwaite behind the net, adding to his already wild reputation.

In one incident last year when the Thunder met the Utah Grizzlies, Lakovic had run a Grizzlies player into the boards on an icing call. As his fallen teammate lay on the ice, goaltender Jamie MacLennan got into it with Lakovic and the two soon began trading punches. After fighting Utah defenseman Barry Nieckar in the ensuing melee, Lakovic got free and, at full speed, nailed MacLennan from behind with a vicious hit, triggering another round of fisticuffs.[32]

Earlier this season, he was on the bench when a drunken fan had dumped his beer on a nearby assistant coach. His teammates averted a full-scale donnybrook by restraining Lakovic from scaling the glass to exact retribution.[33]

A decade later, Lakovic was back in the news when he was charged with assault causing bodily harm and uttering threats after allegedly punching a hotel security guard in the face several times. The guard had been called to Lakovic's room because of noise complaints and had told Lakovic he would be evicted if he and his girlfriend did not keep the noise level down.[34]

Lakovic was but one of many notorious goons to have left an indelible mark on minor-league hockey. Months later, the Moose would try to acquire one of them.

One night after dispatching the Thunder, the Moose laid an egg in front of a nationwide television audience in Canada, losing 3-1 to the abominable Phoenix Roadrunners. The Moose had no answer for a team that had long since been eliminated from the playoff picture and were less than three weeks away from folding.

After another pair of defeats, the Moose returned home and were blown out by the injury-ravaged Detroit Vipers on April Fools' Day. Taped to either side of the Arena's iconic portrait of the Queen that night was a pair of Moose antlers. I would attend 23 games this year and I only wish this game had been one of them, just so I could have seen the antlered Queen.

Less than a week later, the Moose were officially eliminated from playoff contention when they lost both ends of a home-and-home series with the Kansas City Blades. Scoring the game-winner in the first of the two games was former Jets defenseman Jim Kyte. Kyte had been a longtime fixture for the Jets, but he was anything but an offensive dynamo. Over the course of six full seasons in a Jets uniform, he had scored only 11 goals.

The Moose held a pregame awards ceremony before wrapping up their first season in Manitoba with a return engagement against the Blades.

I could only shake my head as I watched Arena staff drape a cheap white cloth over top of a banged-up folding plywood banquet table before arranging the trophies on it. Mark Chipman and team sponsors then handed out the awards with all the pomp and circumstance of the championship trophy presentation in *Slap Shot*. In that timeless scene, the referee called player-coach Reg Dunlop over to the penalty box during a stoppage and barked, "Here you go, ya bum," as he grabbed the trophy from the timekeeper and gruffly handed it off to Dunlop.

Brathwaite took home the top prize as the team's MVP, but he was so visibly hobbled in the warm-up after injuring his knee two nights earlier that the Moose were forced to turn to Riendeau. The seemingly forgotten backup goaltender was so rusty that he could do little but stand in his crease like a cardboard cutout and watch the goals drift past him one by one. The Moose somehow managed to keep the game close, but Riendeau's shoddy goaltending gave them no chance to win and they lost 6-4 to finish with a record of 32-40-10. Only three of the IHL's 19 teams finished below the Moose in the standings.

There is an old saying that you only get one chance to make a good first impression. In this, the Moose had failed utterly. A long playoff run could have gone a long way towards not only firmly establishing the Moose as a fixture on the Winnipeg sports scene but also in healing the stinging wounds left by the Jets' painful departure.

Instead, they would be left with an uphill battle to win over the scorned and skeptical Winnipeg hockey fan. It is a battle the organization would approach with lethargy and indifference.

On the surface, however, the future looked promising. Attendance had picked up late in the year, and financially, there was only a modest loss on operations, a far cry from the situation in Minnesota, where the owners were losing money hand over fist.

Sadly, that promise would quickly fade. A few more wins would be forthcoming, but few would notice or care.

1997-1998: Spinning Wheels

The Moose would enter their second season in Winnipeg having to pick up the pieces of what had been a disastrous campaign a year ago.

"Last year we fell on our face,"[1] admitted head coach and general manager Randy Carlyle, who took over from the deposed Jean Perron on an interim basis in February.

In early June, Moose president and co-owner Mark Chipman began the off-season by making Carlyle's promotion permanent and giving him a new two-year contract.

"Having Randy is very important, critical,"[2] said Chipman.

Carlyle's presence would prove to be far more important to Chipman than to the Moose. An almost father-son bond would develop between the two men that would leave Chipman blind to Carlyle's pedestrian performance behind the bench.

The Moose added Winnipeg native Bruce Southern to the front office as the director of player personnel and parted ways with Frank Serratore, who had been the head coach and general manager during their two seasons in Minnesota.

For the second straight off-season, the Moose would be left with having to build their team from scratch. Only five players from last year were under contract and many of their best players left to sign lucrative contracts with German teams over the summer. Among those to depart were Scott McCrory, their leading scorer, and Jeff Ricciardi, their top defenseman, as well as key contributors Andy Schneider, Eric Dubois and Chris Kontos. They would soon be joined by assistant captain Steve Wilson, a bulwark on the blue line.

Vincent Riendeau, one of the five players that the Moose still had under contract, would also join many of his former teammates in Germany. The Moose bought out the final year of his deal and he would join no fewer than five of his former teammates with the Revier Lions. The Moose had hoped the former NHL netminder would provide them with top-flight goaltending this past season. Instead, he quickly lost his starting position and spent much of the latter half of the year warming the bench.

In total, more than 50 of the IHL's best players would depart for Germany this summer. Import restrictions had been relaxed in the German league, opening the floodgates for its teams to offer tax-free six-figure salaries that IHL teams could not come close to matching. In addition, fewer games and less travel made the German league even more of an attractive destination for the minor-league player.

With so many fewer games, their season ended much sooner, forcing the IHL to adopt a special rule to prevent players whose German league season was over from joining IHL teams for the playoffs. To stop the flood of so-called ringers, any player who had signed in Germany and wanted to return to the IHL that year had to do so before the midway point of the season.

The exodus of players to Germany would become a recurring theme over the next four years and would drain much of the league's top talent. I had once thought the European leagues were at a semiprofessional level and an option a North American player would consider only when he was at the very end of his career. I had fully expected the Moose to lose players to the NHL, but the loss of so many players to the European leagues came as quite a shock.

History buffs may recall that the section of the German World War II–era concentration camp at Auschwitz where the stolen valuables and clothing were sorted and processed was called "Canada." It was so named because the Germans believed that Canada, with its abundant natural resources, was the land of untold riches. So many years later, the roles would be reversed for minor-league hockey players.

It was during this time that I discovered eurohockey.net, an excellent site that provided news on European teams. It would prove to be a far more valuable source of information on tracking current and former IHL players than any other media outlet in North America, and I would become a frequent visitor during the summer months.

In the Expansion Draft, the Moose lost another player when the Grand Rapids Griffins selected promising winger Sean Tallaire. In another odd storyline unique to the IHL, the draft was held a year after their entry into the league, and they were allowed to pluck a player from a woebegotten team they had finished nearly 20 points ahead of.

Randy Gilhen, the subject of so much controversy involving Jean Perron, decided not to stand for the captaincy this year and would soon retire. He would finish out the year as an assistant coach.

As Chipman and Carlyle sought to rebuild the team, they first needed a world-class fighter.

"Carlyle knows that the Moose have lacked stability at one position this season and for 97-98 to become a turnaround year, they must find and sign the most capable fighter they can,"[3] wrote *Free Press* beat writer Tim Campbell.

They had apparently found one in Andy Bezeau, the quintessential goon with a rap sheet that had few equals anywhere in the game.

Bezeau's front teeth had been missing since he was hit with a brick as a teenager. His fingers pointed in different directions because his hand had been broken so often. His nose no longer had any cartilage left, and he had a constant black eye. Behind every bar fight, bench-clearing brawl and court appearance was a hair-raising, off-the-wall story that even the most seasoned hockey fan would have trouble believing. No doubt, a collection of these stories involving Bezeau's exploits could fill an epic novel.

Rick Dudley, one of his former coaches, called Bezeau "the toughest human being I have ever known."[4]

"His appearance was so disheveled that he looked like he just made a break from a chain gang while the warden had a cat nap,"[4] said Steve Ludzik, just after Bezeau had reported to the Muskegon team that Ludzik was coaching.

Last season, Bezeau had racked up 390 penalty minutes, a total that would break records in many leagues. Bezeau, however, had put up that total in just over half a season. The previous year, his total was a whopping 590 penalty minutes.

This was the infamous figure who the Moose acquired via trade from the Fort Wayne Komets in the off-season. As it happened, the Moose and their fans would never get to see Bezeau drop his gloves at the Arena as the IHL, in a rare show of integrity, rejected his contract because it called for a bonus if he set a record for penalty minutes.

Bezeau would move on and spend much of the coming year with the Detroit Vipers, while the Moose had to settle for holdover Craig Johnson. A capable fighter, Johnson was the last of three fighters the Moose had used last season. In that time, he managed to get into four scraps in limited action, but Johnson would be little more than a poor man's substitute for Bezeau and the Moose would soon be in the market for his replacement.

Interestingly, after his playing career, Bezeau would open and run a hockey school in his native Saint John, New Brunswick. Many parents would send their children to learn the finer points of the game from a former player who had piled up 3,521 penalty minutes in 477 pro games.

Among the first legitimate hockey players the Moose would sign over the summer was lanky defenseman Mike Ruark. Ruark's path to the Moose was one of the most unusual and perhaps unprecedented in the annals of pro hockey.

Following two years in the IHL with the Phoenix Roadrunners, Ruark found himself out of work. Figuring his fledgling pro career was all but over, he returned to school, enrolling at the University of Calgary, where he also played for three seasons.

Unlike those in U.S. colleges, most of the players in Canadian colleges were graduates from the junior ranks who were not considered good enough to be pro prospects. It was indeed rare to have anyone from a Canadian college move up to pro hockey, which was why Ruark was so surprised when Carlyle called to offer him a tryout with the Moose.

Nonetheless, Ruark would prove to be a good find for the Moose, and he would be a key member of their defense corps for the next four years.

In addition to re-signing goaltender Fred Brathwaite, the Moose made a number of other additions including defensemen Michael Stewart, Brett Hauer and Marc LaForge and forwards Ralph Intranuovo and Jimmy Roy.

Stewart was a high first-round pick of the New York Rangers seven years earlier who had never made the NHL and was languishing with the Canadian national team. Hauer was entering his fifth pro season and had spent last season with the Chicago Wolves.

Like Ruark, both Stewart and Hauer would be excellent signings, but the same could not be said for LaForge. LaForge was a hard-nosed and frequently suspended journeyman who had become noted for his surly attitude. In one particularly telling incident two years ago while with the Minnesota Moose, he earned a lengthy suspension when he hurled some anti-Semitic remarks at former Jet Mike Hartman, who is Jewish.

Not surprisingly, LaForge would not last long with the Moose. A little homework on their part could easily have prevented this expensive mistake. I had learned of his reputation from reading the IHL e-mail list at plaidworks.com long before the Moose had signed him. I would have thought that the Moose had more comprehensive sources of information on prospective players at their disposal than I did.

Intranuovo was once a highly touted draft pick of the Edmonton Oilers. He had piled up big numbers in junior and in the minor leagues, but he had never been able to stick on an NHL roster. The leading scorer with his AHL team last season, he looked like a great pickup for the Moose. Sadly, I would soon find out why he had not drawn any interest from an NHL organization.

Roy would be perhaps the Moose's most significant addition of the summer. An unheralded player entering his first pro season after spending a year with the Canadian national team, the master agitator would carve out a long career for himself by stirring up trouble. Constantly jawing at opponents and using his stick like a cattle prod, he would become arguably the most hated player in minor-league hockey.

Roy's mouth was so active that a generator hooked up to his jaw could likely have supplied all the electricity needed to run the Arena if there had ever been a power outage during a game.

Jimmy Roy.[1]

He would go on to play nine years in a Moose uniform, and though he would never score much, getting under the skin of his opponents would make him one of the Moose's valuable players. His pugnacious nature would make him a fan favorite, and he would become the team's most recognizable player.

It wouldn't be a proper IHL off-season without a team folding, and this one would be no exception as the Phoenix Roadrunners bit the dust. Undaunted, the league continued to harbor aspirations of future growth. They began to look at new markets in New Orleans, Saskatoon, Victoria and Toronto, but nothing would ever materialize in those cities. The IHL would have enough trouble hanging on to their existing teams.

That task was made even more difficult by the continued loss of NHL affiliations. IHL teams that still had an NHL affiliation were being used as places to stash unwanted veterans rather than to develop prized up-and-coming prospects. Those prospects were instead being sent to the AHL in increasing numbers. The IHL was truly becoming the Independent Hockey League. It would shortly become the Insignificant Hockey League and ultimately the Insolvent Hockey League.

On the ice, the IHL, in consultation with the NHL, adopted some rule changes intended to speed up the game. In his article describing the changes, Scott Taylor of the *Free Press* described Chipman as "the only non-general manager on the IHL's hockey committee."[5] Taylor had a well-earned reputation in Winnipeg as a blowhard, but I never knew about his keen sense of humor before reading that line in his article.

I was more realistic in my expectations for this coming season, but in spite of how bad the Moose had been in their first year, I had seen enough to want to come back. Many other hockey fans in Winnipeg, however, did not share that sentiment. Season ticket sales were down significantly, prompting Chipman to take to the phones himself to call fans asking why they were not renewing.

"We didn't anticipate that we would be, that the attendance would be as difficult to drive as it has been,"[6] he would later say.

Yet practically in the same breath, he would boast about how little the Moose were spending on promotion when compared with some of their IHL brethren.

"We don't have to spend anywhere near the kind of money that Chicago or Houston or Los Angeles or Long Beach have to just to, you know, let people know that they're playing hockey."[6]

He apparently didn't make the obvious connection between the lack of promotion and low attendance. It would be many years before he would begin to understand the reality that minor-league hockey, unlike the NHL, does not sell itself, even in a strong hockey market like Winnipeg.

The Moose's stubborn unwillingness to aggressively market their product would leave them virtually invisible as a corporate entity throughout these early years. The casual fan could be forgiven for not even knowing there was an IHL team in the city.

I often felt as though I was doing more to promote the team on my Web site than the Moose were doing themselves. Still feeling the stinging pain of the loss of the Jets and seeing so little being done by the Moose organization, I took it upon myself to try to encourage fans to support the Moose because I did not want to lose another team.

In one of his many e-mails to me, Rob Gialloreto sharply challenged my notion of the team's lack of visibility in the community. He made no effort to address my points regarding the lack of marketing and instead simply pointed to the time the players spent with children at local community clubs as evidence of his point.

As the Moose continued to give the cold shoulder to the hardcore hockey fan, it would be those children who would become the biggest demographic at the games. In groups of between 10 and 20, they would spend the entire game running off their boundless energy up and down the aisles, back and forth across each row and all through the concourse. They blanketed the cavernous Arena like swarming locusts descending on an orchard in full blossom.

On the back of their invoices, the Moose printed the following statement regarding their ticket policies:

"The Manitoba Moose retain the right to revoke a Ticket purchase due to misuse of the tickets or inconsiderate behavior at the games."

Regrettably, it is a right they would not invoke far too infrequently, if ever.

These 8- to 12-year-old boys would make up anywhere between a third and half of the nightly crowd. Anyone over the age of 12 could have been considered a senior citizen by Moose standards.

To these kids, the game was little more than a background distraction. Even when the Moose scored a goal, few of them noticed. The only exception was when there was an altercation. The first signs of any ill will brought them down to ice level at breakneck speed, where they would pound on the glass and yell, "Fight! Fight! Fight!"

Bringing in so many children may have been part of a long-term strategy to build a future fan base, but their presence would do more to repel ticket-buying fans than to bring in new ones. As attendance plummeted in direct proportion to the average age in the stands, fans would begin pleading for a dedicated "day care" section in the hopes of keeping the kids confined to a particular section. Not surprisingly, those pleas would go unanswered.

I would grow increasingly annoyed not only by these children wreaking havoc with my enjoyment of the game but also by my strong suspicion that they were getting in at a heavily discounted rate while I was paying full price. I should have been the one getting a discount for having to put up with them.

The Moose would use the term "family-oriented" to describe the makeup of the crowds at their games, but families complete with concerned parents were few and far between. Instead, these hordes of children were accompanied by one forlorn adult who looked as though he would rather have been selected for jury duty than be sitting at the game. I would often spot this "token adult," or "T.A.," sitting off by himself curled up reading a book or nodding off. The Moose would never have high-scoring teams, so their ear-splitting goal horn generally did not pose any problem for the particularly weary T.A. who needed to catch a few winks.

The T.A. was generally a balding, middle-aged man with a five o'clock shadow dusting the double chin of a weather-beaten face that had seen one too many harsh Manitoba winters. Bored out of his mind, he was the antithesis of the children he was there to nominally supervise. Utterly devoid of enthusiasm and energy, pulling himself up out of his seat was a struggle that would make scaling Mount Everest look easy by comparison.

The prototypical T.A. had much in common with the remaining half to two-thirds of a representative crowd at a Moose game, where the lack of passion was palpable on most nights.

Winnipeg fans, as in many Canadian cities, were notorious for being quieter than their American counterparts, but although the atmosphere at Jets games was also relatively serene, fans clearly were interested. It was the exact opposite atmosphere at a Moose game. No one cared if the team won or lost. Apathy reigned.

Moose goals would bring some obligatory applause, and the shrill from the screaming children would raise the decibel level even higher when there was a fight. During the rest of the time, however, I would hear more noise at the library while doing research for this book than I heard at most games.

As I scanned the lower bowl during games, I would often wonder why so many of these disinterested over-12s even bothered to come. Perhaps it was a case of wives kicking their husbands out of the house for the night or the absence of anything good on television that evening. Whatever the reason, the Moose clearly weren't filling the void for these semicomatose "fans," or "stakeholders," a term Chipman would coin when referring to his customers.

I would scoff each time Chipman would use that term, either in letters to season ticket holders or in radio or television interviews.

Though I had an increasing emotional investment, I held no financial stake in the team.

The malaise that permeated throughout the stands was no less evident in the paid staffers working the souvenir stands or the ushers. They would spend the evening lazily chatting with each other and almost seemed offended when a passing customer dared to interrupt their conversation.

There was one rare exception when an usher broke from tradition and ran after me as I headed up the stairs. He demanded to see my ticket and then acted like he was doing me a favor by pointing out where my seat was, almost like he was looking for a tip. To avoid the risk of such unwanted encounters in the future, I would take the escalators to the upper deck, where no ushers were stationed, and then walk down to my seat.

An equally disturbing trend at the games was that the prime seats were often just as sparsely populated as those in the upper reaches. The few fans who were in attendance were buying the much cheaper tickets rather than spending the extra money to sit close to the ice, further adding to the Moose's financial woes.

In the years that followed the Jets' departure, Winnipeg fans had been criticized, with some validity, for not supporting the team well enough. Tickets were, indeed, generally available and few games had sold out, but most of those unsold tickets were in the upper deck or in the nosebleed sections. Nearly all the most expensive seats in the house were always sold, and throughout my two decades of attending Jets games, I was never once able to sit close to the bench.

Once again, it would be the exact opposite at Moose games. There were many occasions in which I would walk up to the box office as late as an hour before the game and have my choice of seats anywhere within a stone's throw of the bench. In the coming years, when I wanted to sit at ice level, I would simply buy a ticket in the cheap seats and take my place in the front row. No one checked my ticket. No one cared. Security was so lax that I could have opened the swinging door that separated the end of the bench from the seating area and sat right next to a Moose player.

I was not the only person to take advantage of this informal free seat upgrade program and move down. A time-lapse video showing the stands during the first period might have looked like a foraging group of army ants converging on the lower bowl.

One of the more memorable of such games came when I was in the front row only a few seats away from the end of the Moose bench to my right. While chatting with another fan who had also moved down from the cheap seats, I glanced over and noticed a collection of scruffy characters staggering down the aisle, looking as if they had just crawled out of a dumpster. I saw their unshaven faces and caught a whiff of the month-old garbage they had been sleeping in as they shuffled past me on their way towards the bench.

After sitting down, they unzipped their tattered parkas, pulled out some canisters from their pockets and poured a golden-colored beverage with a white, foamy head into plastic cups.

"What do you suppose that is?" asked the guy to my left with an obvious look of sarcasm on his face.

"Apple juice," I replied.

We both laughed.

Parked in the best seats in the house, they spent the rest of the evening getting plastered. I doubt if they even knew a game was going on.

Arena policies prohibited outside food and especially outside liquor. At Moose games, however, it was a case of anything goes. It would be far from the last time I would notice patrons taking advantage of the laissez-faire atmosphere, and one particular incident would later affect me very personally.

The Manitoba Moose opened their second training camp at the River Heights Community Center under considerably less fanfare than they had a year earlier. The Moose played only three exhibition games, all against the semipro Canadian national team, and won only once. In the only real drama of camp, Craig Johnson fended off challenger Louis Bedard to hold on to the job as the Moose's fighter for the time being.

Days before the regular-season opener, the Moose re-signed Greg Pankewicz, who had led the team in both goals and temper tantrums last year. Rather than try his luck in Germany like most of his ex-teammates, the volatile Pankewicz tried out with the NHL's Calgary Flames. He had been impressive in Flames camp, but he opted to return to the Moose rather than accept an assignment to Calgary's farm team in Saint John.

"I know what to expect from him and we like what Greg Pankewicz brought to our hockey team,"[7] said Carlyle.

"He'll be a key member of our hockey club and he'll be an ambassador for our city."[8]

Pankewicz would indeed prove to be a key member of the Moose this year, but once again, the door to the penalty box at the Arena would take just as much of a beating as the statistics of the goaltenders he faced. The increasingly empty stands would serve only to amplify the echo that would reverberate around the Arena after Pankewicz's many door-slamming tirades.

The Moose also added centermen Brad Purdie and Brett Punchard. In his second full season of pro hockey, Purdie would place among the Moose's top scorers, and would prove to be a shrewd acquisition. Punchard, meanwhile, would do little for the team, but he would go into the history books as having the most appropriate surname for a member of the "Fighting" Moose. Oddly, Punchard never did get into a scrap while with the Moose.

The Moose officially kicked off their second season on Thursday, October 2, in an ominous fashion with a 3-0 loss to the Chicago Wolves at the half-empty Arena. For the second straight year, the Moose were shut out in their home opener, and the only cheers of the night came during the pregame introductions as the crowd saluted members of the 1972 Team Canada squad. Wendell Young, well on his way to nemesis status with the Moose, was forced to make some good stops, but all in all, it would be a relatively easy shutout for him.

As I wrote after the game, "For the most part though, this talent-challenged team may be in for a long year if this game was any indication of the way the season will go."[10]

Sadly, my early premonition would prove accurate.

In addition to their reconstructed roster, the Moose also debuted Stacey Nattrass, their new anthem singer. A choir teacher by day and jazz vocalist by night, her performances were, by and large, about as mediocre as the team she was singing for. There was little chance that she was going to make anyone forget such legendary voices as Wayne Messmer in Chicago or Roger Doucet in Montreal.

She would be most noted for drawing attention to herself by strutting out in a low-cut, shiny-sequined gown that was better suited for a night club than an audience of young children at a hockey game. I could only shake my head and wonder who she was trying to impress. Rob Gialloreto would later staunchly defend her nightly choice of garb that so flagrantly flew in the face of the organization's efforts to promote a family-friendly atmosphere.

Oddly, Nattrass would later say, "For the most part, I live pretty anonymously."[9]

During these years, despite her best efforts to the contrary, it was not possible to be more anonymous than to be seen at a Moose game.

Before taking on Kansas City the following Thursday, the Moose added a pair of 24-year-olds – winger Mark Kolesar and goaltender Rich Parent. Kolesar was a native of Neepawa, Manitoba, a two-hour drive from Winnipeg, who had spent the past three years shuttling between the Toronto Maple Leafs and their farm team in St. John's. Described as a good skater with speed and a scoring touch, he would spend much of his time with the Moose in Carlyle's doghouse and do nothing to help the team's offensive woes.

"I'd just like to see him battle harder"[11] would be a familiar theme echoed by Carlyle.

On the surface, it appeared as though the Moose had struck gold with Parent. He had been the IHL's outstanding goaltender last year in leading the Detroit Vipers to their first Turner Cup. Combined with Fred Brathwaite, it looked like a formidable duo that could make even the offensively challenged Moose a championship contender.

Though Parent would be anything but a bust, it wouldn't quite work out that way. Rather than striking gold, it would be more like rusty tin.

Both Kolesar and Parent had simply been loaned to the Moose from their respective NHL organizations. To my amazement, the Moose did not have to give up any players, draft picks or cash.

IHL teams, including the Moose, would regularly pick up veteran players like this from an NHL organization or its AHL affiliate. AHL teams were restricted in the number of veterans they could dress, and when faced with an excess, they would often place them with a willing IHL team or even a rival AHL team. The parent NHL organization would benefit not only by offloading the cost of the player's salary but also by freeing up roster spots for their younger prospects.

Goaltenders were often especially targeted for an IHL assignment. Many NHL organizations had an established NHL-worthy veteran in their system as well as a younger developing prospect, and both needed to play often. In the case of the veteran, since he would be the first to be recalled in case of an injury, he needed the playing time to remain sharp. The younger player, however, also needed the playing time in order to develop his skills at the pro level.

Since both could not play regularly on the same team, the veteran would often be loaned out to an IHL club. For this reason, goaltending became a real strength of the IHL in its later years.

Not only could spare talent be readily found from NHL organizations, but quality players could often be had for virtually nothing from other minor-league teams, even within the same league.

A common scenario within the IHL would be a team at the bottom of the standings and/or on the verge of folding looking to unload its top players to anyone willing to pay their salaries. A bidding war would ensue only if there were multiple takers.

The relative ease with which a minor-league team could acquire players like this would continue to astound me. In major leagues like the WHA and NHL, it was dog-eat-dog as rival general managers engaged in bitter horse trading like stockbrokers on the floor of the New York Stock Exchange. Assets were jealously guarded, and nothing was given away for free.

This ready access to available talent would make the Moose's on-ice failures during their IHL years look even worse. An IHL team that was truly committed to winning could do so much easier than an NHL team could.

The Moose picked up their first win of the year in front of a second consecutive paltry gathering at the Arena on Thursday night. Pankewicz led the Moose with a hat trick, including the game-winner late in the third period, but the game's strangest goal came midway through the third with the Moose trailing 3-2. From his own blue line, Purdie shot the puck down the ice and went off for a line change. As he was taking his place on the bench, goaltender Jon Casey mishandled the puck and it went into the net, tying the score.

Two nights later in Milwaukee, Ralph Intranuovo emerged from virtual hibernation to score three times, and Fred Brathwaite was again stellar in backstopping the Moose to their second straight win. That pattern of flashes of brilliance sandwiched by long periods of invisibility would define Intranuovo's tenure with the Moose.

I watched in awe many nights as the tiny jitterbug skated figure eights around befuddled defenders. The first time I had seen him dazzle the crowd, I was amazed as to why someone who had such a tremendous skill set was languishing in the minor leagues and not starring in the NHL.

I would soon see why: On most nights, he would practically vanish into thin air. So often on the way home from games, I would wonder if he had even played. Harry Houdini could not have pulled off a better disappearing act.

Intranuovo would remind me of former Jet Andrew McBain, a one-time highly touted first-round draft choice whom I had seen so often while I was a Jets season ticket holder. Much like Intranuovo, McBain was blessed with immense talent, but he earned the scorn of Jets fans for his inability to parlay those skills into a more successful career. Long after the Jets had left Winnipeg, McBain would be remembered as the biggest underachiever in team history.

It was easy to see why NHL scouts had drooled over Intranuovo at the junior level and why he was once such a highly regarded prospect. Though he would put up some good numbers in the minor leagues, his impact on the game was anything but inspiring. He was another player whose lasting legacy would be one of disappointment.

The Moose flew on to Orlando, where they split a pair of games. Brathwaite stood on his head to enable the Moose to take the opener, but he couldn't replicate his heroics in the finale, enabling Parent to see his first action since joining the Moose.

In between the two games, the Moose signed 34-year-old free-agent centerman Mike Ridley and traded Russ Romaniuk to Long Beach for rugged defenseman Brian Chapman.

A Winnipeg native and a 12-year NHL veteran, Ridley was trying to make a comeback with the Moose following an injury-riddled season a year ago. He scored in his first game, but injuries would continue to plague him, forcing him to end his comeback after only three weeks.

The trade would be by far the more impactful transaction of the two.

Like Ridley, Romaniuk was coming off a season marred by an endless series of injuries. His year began with an eye injury and ended with an enlarged spleen and a case of mononucleosis. The Moose offered him a cut-rate deal over the summer, but the rival Blades stepped up and offered him a lucrative two-year deal that the Moose were forced to match.

For the second consecutive year, the Moose were able to offload an underperforming, high-salaried player to Long Beach. This time, however, it would be the Moose who would get the better part of the deal. After a quick start with his new team, Romaniuk's production would tail off and he would finish the year with Las Vegas.

For his part, Romaniuk was disappointed to be leaving his hometown team.

"I really see an exciting team developing in Manitoba and I wanted badly to be a part of that."[12]

He need not have shed any tears as he wouldn't miss much.

Chapman was a 29-year-old veteran who had been through the wars with four different minor-league teams since turning pro a decade earlier. Aside from a three-game stint with the Hartford Whalers six years ago, he had spent his entire pro career in the minors.

What appeared to be the pickup of a run-of-the-mill journeyman, however, would turn into much more as Chapman would eventually become the greatest defenseman in Moose history.

Chapman was not blessed with blazing speed, but he was as tough and ornery as anyone in the game. He played like a cantankerous old fart and made life miserable for any opposing forwards who dared to venture into his territory. He took care of his own end of the ice as if his next meal depended on it, and there would be no one more well-respected in the dressing room.

If Chapman were a car, he'd be your father's brown Chevy station wagon. It's old. It coughs. It sputters. It's rusting on the bottom. Sometimes it misfires. You're probably embarrassed to be seen in it. But it gets you where you're going and you can count on it. It's probably more reliable than your neighbor's Ferrari, and you didn't have to take out a second mortgage on your house to pay for it.

Brian Chapman.[1]

Not unlike many hockey players, he also had quite the potty mouth. He showed it off to me personally one night when I was seated in the front row along the glass.

"That was f---ing offside," yelled Chapman at a linesman as he skated by.

From then on, I would refer to him as Brian F. Chapman.

Back home at the Arena, the Moose lost their second straight when they dropped a gut-wrenching 5-4 decision to Romaniuk and the Ice Dogs. After the Moose rallied from a two-goal deficit to tie the game in the third period, the visitors scored with just over a minute to play to send the Moose down to defeat.

Most of the action, however, came late in the first period when two separate altercations four seconds apart filled the penalty boxes. In the second melee, Marc LaForge jumped in during a scrap and earned not one but two game misconducts in what would be his lone shining moment as a member of the "Fighting" Moose.

The Moose took two of three games on the road to even their record at 5-5-0 before returning home to host the Solar Bears in a pair of games over the weekend that kicked off a five-game home stand. Before the opener, the Moose added rangy 22-year-old former Detroit Viper and current Ottawa Senators prospect Radim Bicanek to fill in on the blue line for an injured Dale DeGray.

The Vipers had a partial affiliation agreement with the Senators until a sudden and messy divorce prompted Ottawa to hastily reassign all five prospects they had placed in Detroit to other minor-league clubs. Bicanek was one of those prospects, and the Moose became one of the beneficiaries of that divorce.

It would be another example of how easily top-caliber talent could simply fall into a team's lap at this level. Though he would never develop into an NHL star, Bicanek was an effective player who would make a major contribution at both ends of the rink. He would also be one of the few bona fide NHL prospects the Moose would have during their IHL years.

The bitter divorce between the Vipers and Senators was a sad sign of the times as relations between the two leagues continued to deteriorate. The competing priorities of winning and development were not mixing well, and this would not be the last midseason divorce between an IHL and NHL team.

The Moose began the home stand with an epic display of offensive futility in a 4-1 loss. Overshadowing the final score, however, was a second-period incident in which Eric Nickulas blindsided Jimmy Roy with a vicious elbow and knocked him out cold. Roy suffered two concussions on the play, one when he was hit by Nickulas's elbow, the other when he hit the ice.

There was an eerie silence in the crowd as Roy lay motionless in a pool of his own blood before he was eventually carried off the ice on a stretcher. A few minutes later, a call came over the P.A. system for any doctors in the crowd to report to the Moose dressing room immediately.

As concerned as I was for Roy's well-being, I was shocked that the Moose did not have a doctor available on standby. According to their media guide, the Moose actually had three team physicians, and it seemed natural to have at least one of them there, particularly since it had become a long-accepted practice to have an ambulance ready and waiting at each game.

Roy would have convulsions and had almost swallowed his tongue, but fortunately, after a stay at St. Boniface Hospital, he was given a clean bill of health. He would return to the lineup in a couple of weeks just as feisty as ever.

For the hit, Nickulas received an elbowing major and a game misconduct. Though the penalties may appear to be an obvious result, when it came to officiating in the IHL, as Jean Perron had stated soon after he was hired, it was an adventure like nothing other in the game. Even the most straightforward calls were frequently missed as officials were either out of position or looking elsewhere.

The hit-and-miss nature of IHL officiating would also often allow players who had committed acts such as this to avoid suspension. If none of the officials had seen the incident, there would be no way for the league to properly assess the severity, since, unlike the NHL, footage of the game was rarely, if ever, available.

Lost in all the furor involving Roy and Nickulas was the compelling story of Orlando winger Kevin Smyth, who had made his first appearance at the Arena on this night. A year earlier in a game against the Indianapolis Ice, Smyth was struck in the right eye by a deflected puck, suffering permanent vision loss. Three months later, Smyth was back on the ice, making one of the most remarkable comebacks in sports history. Fittingly, his first-period goal against the Moose proved to be the game-winner.

Before an announced crowd of just over 4,000 who braved an early-season winter storm, the Moose salvaged a split of the two-game set with a 5-2 victory. Unfortunately, the game cost the Moose the services of another player when Orlando defenseman Barry Dreger stabbed Dave Thomlinson in the back of the knee with his stick. The hard-nosed veteran whom the Moose had signed in the off-season suffered knee ligament damage and would be out of the lineup for a month. Not unexpectedly, all three officials missed the play, and Dreger's infraction would go unpunished.

After another shootout loss at the hands of Danny Lorenz and the Admirals, the Moose prepared to entertain the Blades in the first of what would be an eventful, but again, sparsely attended, pair of games.

On the morning of Friday's opener, the Blues recalled Rich Parent to replace an injured Grant Fuhr, leaving the Moose to scramble to find a backup for Fred Brathwaite. Unable to find a replacement from the pro ranks in time for the game, the Moose had to turn to 35-year-old meat inspector Bob Brisebois from nearby Île des Chênes.

A goaltender in the Hanover-Tache Hockey League (HTHL), a regional senior circuit, Brisebois was on his day off from his regular job when he got the call from the Moose. At first, he thought it was a practical joke, but the Moose were indeed serious. Brisebois was on the bench in full uniform that night backing up Brathwaite and watched the Moose rally for a 5-4 shootout victory.

This was not the first or the last time in the annals of minor-league hockey that an amateur goaltender would be called upon.

Less than two weeks later in Quebec, 32-year-old police officer Steve Carrier not only had to suit up but actually play. Without both of their regular goaltenders, the Michigan K-Wings had summoned Martin Legault from the East Coast Hockey League (ECHL), but his flight was delayed, forcing them to turn to Carrier in the game's opening minutes.

The K-Wings formed a protective shield around Carrier, holding the Rafales to one shot that Carrier stopped, until Legault finally arrived, "scrambling to the bench in half-uniform."[13] The Rafales went on to win the game 4-3, but the K-Wings let Carrier keep his game jersey as a memento of the unforgettable occasion.

Just one week later, the Utah Grizzlies turned to their front office and suited up executive vice president Tim Mouser as their emergency backup goaltender. Fortunately, in this case, Mouser did not actually have to play.

In later years, I would be surprised to learn that, even in the WHA, a major pro league close to being on par with the NHL, amateur goaltenders were used with surprising regularity. During their seven seasons in the WHA, for example, the Jets had suited up an amateur goaltender on three separate occasions. The most notable such occasion came in 1976 when Andy Stoesz backed up Curt Larsson in a playoff game after starter Joe Daley had been suspended.

The Moose at last found a professional goaltender to serve as Brathwaite's backup, but the Blades turned the tables in the finale and scored two late goals to hand the Moose a 4-3 defeat. Once again, however, the loss was overshadowed by a scary incident involving a Moose player.

Louis Dumont went headfirst into the boards and was motionless on the ice for several minutes until he was taken off on a stretcher. Coincidentally, Dumont had been recalled from the ECHL last week to replace the injured Roy, who himself was taken off on a stretcher to begin the home stand. Like Roy, however, after a short stay in a local hospital, he too would be given a clean bill of health and return to action.

Dumont was but one of many so-called "coasties" who would come and go as the Moose, not unlike other IHL teams, used the ECHL as a free farm system. Working for little more than subsistence wages at the lowest level of organized pro hockey, these eager youngsters would jump at the chance to make an impression in the IHL. Most of them, like Dumont, would play only a handful of games for the Moose, but some would stick for longer periods and make a valuable contribution. Whether it was for an injury replacement or to provide a boost of energy to a sagging lineup, the pipeline of players from the ECHL would prove vital to the Moose during their years in the IHL.

After hovering around the .500 mark for the first month of the season, the Moose lost seven of their next nine games. New additions Rick Girard and Jason Christie as well as the return of Jimmy Roy to the lineup failed to stem the downward spiral as the Moose entered the month of December with the second-worst record in the Western Conference.

The low point of their most recent slide came in Kansas City, where they were blown out by a score of 6-0 in an intense, fight-filled affair. This game would sow the seeds of what would become a vicious, guttural rivalry over the next three years. Many of the games between the two clubs would degenerate into hostile grudge matches that would take on the look of tag-team wrestling.

The reeling Moose returned home to begin a 12-game home stand with a sense of urgency.

"We have to build something out of this home stand,"[14] said Carlyle following an hour-long closed-door meeting with the players.

Instead, the Moose would only hold themselves above water and enter the new year ahead of just the floundering San Antonio Dragons in the West. Though that mark was still good enough to put the Moose in a playoff position, their record was only marginally better than what it had been at the same time last year.

The Moose began the home stand with an embarrassing loss to the lowly Rafales before struggling to beat a Thunder team so shorthanded that their coach had to suit up and take a regular shift.

The enigmatic Ralph Intranuovo saw his most recent goal-scoring drought reach an amazing 14 games. He finally scored in a loss to the Vipers in which legendary goon Andy Bezeau netted the winning goal. That evening, I rode home on the bus with a Moose usher who said, "The Moose suck. It's a big 'whoop-de-doo' when they actually score a goal."[10]

Desperate for some offensive punch, the Moose broke open the piggy bank to sign winger Joe Frederick, the Admirals' leading scorer. Frederick's 25-game tryout contract with Milwaukee had expired, and the Moose outbid several teams to secure his services. A key factor in Frederick's decision was a call from Chapman, who convinced his former teammate in Phoenix to join the Moose.

Frederick would score twice in his first game with the Moose, but though he would rack up some decent numbers, he would not make nearly the same impact he had made during his brief stay in Milwaukee.

Meanwhile, the team continued to struggle both on the ice and at the gate. Even with the infusion of 9,000 complimentary vouchers given to season ticket holders for the December games, crowds remained alarmingly sparse throughout the home stand.

The lone exception was the sellout on New Year's Eve. Playing on New Year's Eve had become a popular Winnipeg tradition for the past decade, and it was clearly the only reason for the large crowd. A defiant Rob Gialloreto, however, saw it differently:

"To me, 10,000 fans indicates the trend of increased attendance."[15]

Not surprisingly, this "trend" would last only one game. The home stand ended two nights later before an announced crowd of 5,862.

In another attempt to bolster their sagging fortunes, the Moose made a deal before hitting the road. They traded Dale DeGray and the recently signed Rick Girard to Quebec in exchange for centerman Michel Mongeau, defenseman Jeff Parrott and fighter Craig Martin.

Mongeau, a minor-league journeyman, and Parrott, an unheralded player, would both become important additions and Martin, unlike Darin Kimble last year, would have no difficulties finding opponents. He would rack up an impressive total of 15 fights over the latter half of the season.

The Moose dropped the opener of a pair of games in Chicago, but they rebounded for a 4-1 win in the finale, marking their first victory in seven meetings with the Wolves this season. Sadly, that lack of success against Chicago would be a recurring theme for years to come and sow the seeds of another rivalry.

This rivalry, however, would be very different from the one they were developing with Kansas City. There would be some ugly moments, but for the most part, the two teams would stick to hockey. Their games would be intense, hotly contested and highly entertaining, but the Moose almost always found themselves on the losing end. It would be a one-way rivalry.

Years later, Judd Sirott, Chicago's broadcaster and director of media relations, would state, "The Wolves own this Manitoba franchise and they know it."[16]

It would be impossible to argue his point. Combined with their success this year, the Wolves would post a record of 23-9-3 against the Moose in regular-season play and win 10 of the 12 playoff games between the two teams over the next three years.

The Wolves did not just save their best for the Moose. In the IHL's final years, the Wolves would become the league's standard-bearers, the bullies who chased everyone else off the playground. "Anybody but Chicago" would soon become the favorite team of fans around the league come playoff time.

As hated as the Wolves would become, however, they would also be quietly admired and respected. Starting with ownership, they showed a determination to win that was unequaled anywhere in the league during these years.

Led by general manager Kevin Cheveldayoff and fiery coach John Anderson, described as the "league's champion door-slammer,"[17] the Wolves spared no expense in bringing in the best players. There was a salary cap in the IHL, but there were few consequences for violating it. So they did. The end result would be two Turner Cup championships and another appearance in the finals.

Interestingly, years later, after Chipman had acquired an NHL franchise, Cheveldayoff would move north to become Chipman's top assistant.

Chicago's formula of bringing in the NHL's prime cast-offs would not work for most IHL clubs. Many of these one-time elite NHL players who had been assigned to the minors, often for the first time in their careers, would sulk at the demotion and be anything but a positive addition.

It was very different with the Wolves. Their recruits did not mope and instead were major contributors to highly successful teams.

These Wolves teams were likely as good as or even better than the four expansion teams the NHL would add during the coming years. The talent pool in the new 30-team NHL would become so diluted that many of its lower-echelon teams were largely made up of IHL-caliber players. I would regularly refer to the hapless New York Islanders as the "IHL-anders" and the perennially weak Minnesota Wild as the "W-IHL-d." Following the IHL's demise, I would often remark that the IHL didn't fold; rather, it was just absorbed into the NHL.

The Moose went on a bit of a roll early in the new year, but it wouldn't take long for them to fall back into their more customary purgatorial state, still mired near the bottom of the league standings.

With just over a minute to play in a tied game against the Blades at the Arena, Steve Jaques drew Greg Pankewicz into a scuffle, and the two went off for coincidental roughing minors. At the time, it seemed relatively inconsequential, but as I was quick to discover, players who had penalty time remaining at the end of regulation were ineligible to participate in the shootout. It was a brilliant move by Jaques to give his team a decided advantage in the penalty-shot contest that followed.

Pankewicz's reputation around the league as a hothead would make him the target of other agitators seeking to either take him off the ice during a critical moment of a game or keep him out of a potential shootout. It was only the agitator's fear that he would draw the lone penalty and give the Moose a power play that would keep this bit of gamesmanship from becoming even more popular with opposing teams.

Scoring in the shootout that evening was defenseman Michael Stewart, a surprising choice by the Moose to be one of the shooters. Stewart was not much of an offensive threat, but with Pankewicz in the penalty box and so few other quality snipers available to him, a desperate Carlyle was forced to look at less conventional options. Throughout his time with the Moose, however, Stewart would reward his coach's confidence by becoming one of the team's most effective shooters, scoring on more than a third of his opportunities.

In late January, the Moose broke a five-game losing streak thanks to some spectacular goaltending from Fred Brathwaite and a late goal off the stick of defenseman Mike Ruark, perhaps the most unlikely of heroes.

It was the first and only goal of the season for Ruark, who was arguably the clumsiest puckhandler on the team. From a distance, he looked like an awkward, hunchbacked figure, so top heavy he might topple over. Yet he would become arguably the Moose's most dependable blueliner. He backed down from no one and was often the only player left standing in a scramble near the Moose goal.

He wasn't quite the Rock of Gibraltar, but he was the big oak tree in your front yard that didn't buckle when your neighbor's teenage son crashed his father's car into it. It may have lost a little bark, but the tree remained firmly rooted and intact while the wrecker came to salvage what was left of the car.

Carlyle would later say, "I think he's become Mr. Reliable for us. He's a guy, if you look at it all, whose mistakes have become minimal."[18]

Ruark would also do his part with the fisticuffs. His total of 44 fights would lead the Moose all-time during their years in the IHL.

Before leaving to begin an epic eight-game, two-week road trip, the Moose dropped a gut-wrenching 2-1 decision to Kansas City that featured more stickwork than goals. Pankewicz was again the target of the visiting Blades, and their strategy would pay off handsomely. With the Moose buzzing around the Blades' goal in the dying seconds, Pankewicz took a silly retaliation penalty when he laid a wicked two-handed slash on defenseman Shawn Heins, all but ending the Moose's comeback hopes.

"Greg Pankewicz is the type of player that can make a difference,"[19] said Carlyle about his top scorer.

Regrettably, that difference would not always be a positive one.

The Moose split a pair of games in Indianapolis that featured no fewer than eight fights over the two contests. Craig Martin was ejected in the opener after Steve McLaren had hopped off the bench to fight him during a line change. Not only was McLaren suspended for coming off the bench to start a fight, but Martin would also be suspended, since excess players on the ice were not allowed to get involved in an altercation. Chipman, a lawyer by trade, would later personally argue Martin's appeal to no avail. I was unhappy that Martin had to serve a suspension, but I was pleasantly surprised that, even in the fight-happy IHL, they had some semblance of moral standards.

The day after the weekend set in Indianapolis, the Moose returned Mark Kolesar to the Leafs, who, in turn, loaned him to the AHL's Hamilton Bulldogs, the Oilers' farm team. Kolesar had but one goal to show for his bitterly disappointing tenure with the Moose and had been relegated to spot duty, seeing regular ice time only when the Moose had a rash of injuries.

In return for Kolesar, the Bulldogs loaned 23-year-old Bill Bowler to the Moose. It would barely warrant any ink in the pages of the *Free Press*, but it would be one of the most significant additions in team history.

Described as a "shifty playmaker,"[20] Bowler had been dominant in the junior ranks, but he had never been drafted by an NHL team. He had signed a free-agent contract with the Oilers this past summer, but after failing to crack their lineup, he was assigned to Hamilton, where he struggled with only 31 points in 46 games.

Not lacking for skills, the 5-foot-9 Bowler was thought to be small for the NHL. Indeed, despite his ability to skate rings around his adversaries, during this era, he would often have been run over by his much larger opponents. It would not be until years later, when the NHL had finally instituted crackdowns on obstruction penalties, that the league would become more friendly to the smaller, skilled player like Bowler. Unfortunately, these rule changes would come too late for him, but looking back, I would often wonder if Bowler would have been able to flourish under those new rules. No doubt, it is a question he has asked himself as well.

In that environment, Bowler likely would have carved out a very successful career for himself at the game's highest level. Instead, he would have to settle for becoming the most skilled offensive player in Moose history. He would often remind me of Ralph Intranuovo as he weaved his magic in the opponent's end of the rink, but unlike Intranuovo, he was a player I would notice almost every night.

Bowler scored in his first game with the Moose, but his new team continued to tread water heading into the All-Star break. Pankewicz was the Moose's only representative at the All-Star Game, and he scored twice and added an assist to make his first All-Star appearance a memorable one. He registered the second-hardest shot in the skills competition, but he would have won hands down if there had been a competition for the biggest temper.

Before kicking off a pair of games against the Utah Grizzlies at the Arena, the Moose made another deal, sending goaltender Rich Parent back to the Vipers for 28-year-old winger Scott Thomas and 24-year-old goaltender Johan Hedberg.

Thomas was a minor-league veteran who had scored 30 or more goals in three of the past five seasons and would prove to be the perfect complement to Bowler. Hedberg would join the Moose shortly after the Olympic Games in Nagano, Japan, where he was serving as the third goaltender for the Swedish team. Though he was almost a throw-in in the deal, he would go on to become the most renowned player in Moose history.

"I've heard Winnipeg is a good hockey town,"[21] he would say soon after his arrival. He was right. It just wasn't a good Moose town.

Backed by another brilliant outing from Brathwaite, the Moose escaped with a 3-2 victory in the opener, then they coasted to a 9-2 win the following evening to complete the sweep over Utah.

The Moose would be anything but a top-flight contender during their years in the IHL, but they would have regularly finished among the league leaders if they only had more games with Utah on their schedule. Whether the Grizzlies, as they were on this weekend, were near the top of the standings or near the bottom, the Moose would handle them with ease.

The following day, the Moose held their second annual Sports Carnival to raise funds for the Yearling Foundation, the Moose's community service arm that supported children's charities. Had I known that Chipman was going to take a turn in the dunk tank, it would have been worth far more than the $5 entrance fee for me to attend.

Bolstered by their new additions, the Moose slowly began to show signs of improvement. The duo of Bowler and Thomas quickly became an offensive force, and Hedberg got off to a hot start with a shutout in his first full game with the Moose. They were able to put some distance between themselves and the hapless Dragons and even passed the injury-riddled Thunder to move into seventh place in the West.

"Our team is playing with a lot of confidence,"[22] said Brad Purdie as the Moose flew home to begin a season-ending 11-game home stand in mid-March.

Sadly, that confidence would soon fade away.

The home stand began with two frustrating losses to the Admirals followed by another pair of defeats at the hands of the Fort Wayne Komets. The newfound scoring punch disappeared and the goaltending tandem of Brathwaite and Hedberg began to falter. In addition, Greg Pankewicz kept blowing his stack, taking a number of needless penalties that hurt the Moose badly.

"It's just the way I am ... I'm on the edge all the time,"[23] said Pankewicz after yet another temper tantrum that cost the Moose their fourth straight defeat.

The Moose, however, clinched their first playoff berth since moving to Winnipeg thanks to the faltering San Antonio Dragons, who came in for a pair of games over the weekend to close out the month of March.

The Dragons, after a first-place finish in the Midwest Division last year, had fallen on hard times this year and persisting rumors of their imminent demise would be made official weeks later. As they had last year, however, they remained among the league leaders in penalty minutes. Led by former NHL tough guy Jeff Brubaker, they were derisively known as the "Dragoons" among fans around the league.

They had no shortage of players willing to drop the gloves, much like their coach during his playing days. However, their penalty minute leader, Daniel Shank, was anything but the prototypical boxer on skates normally associated with a high penalty total.

A diminutive, eccentric minor-league journeyman, Shank was an intense competitor known, like Pankewicz, for his temper tantrums, but also for being an agitator. A favorite tactic of his would be to pick a fight and then run away or drop to his knees and cover his head just after his would-be adversary had dropped his gloves.

He would succeed in drawing plenty of calls against opposing players, but he would take even more himself, making himself hated not only by opponents but by his own teammates as well.

"In all my decades of hockey, Shank was the most disruptive player I had ever seen on a team,"[24] said Glen Sonmor, the Minnesota Moose's director of player development, just after the Moose had released Shank.

It was quite the condemnation from Sonmor, a man who had presided over the biggest cadre of thugs and goons the game had ever known while behind the bench of the WHA's Birmingham Bulls two decades earlier. The Bulls' roster featured such clowns as Steve Durbano, Gilles "Bad News" Bilodeau, Phil Roberto and Frank "Seldom" Beaton. It was a collection that still inspires equal parts fear, disdain, laughter and embarrassment to this day from fans and players who lived through those years.

Shank was no less hated by fans around the league. The mere mention of his name would send the modem lights flickering with the intensity of a siren atop a speeding ambulance. Since Shank had more stickers on his suitcase than a travel agent, seemingly everyone in cyberspace had a Daniel Shank story all their own. Among the most bizarre was an unconfirmed report that Shank used to tap each end of his stick after a goal and begin jabbering in fake Chinese.

All told, Daniel Shank would go down in history as one of the most infamous characters in the annals of minor-league hockey.

After playing in Quebec the previous night, Shank and the Dragons arrived in Winnipeg the next morning. Unfortunately, most of their equipment was on a different flight and wouldn't arrive until well into the evening, delaying the start of the game for more than an hour. The Moose, however, didn't make an announcement about the delayed start until close to the regularly scheduled start time, leaving those of us in the stands to wonder what was happening.

While waiting, I was joined by my good friend Steve, his wife Kathy and his brother John, who collectively quadrupled the population in my section. More accustomed to seeing larger crowds for the Jets, Kathy looked around and made the observation, "What a poor crowd."

Her husband quickly corrected her.

"No, this is a *good* crowd."

Steve was right. The announced attendance for this game was 7,322, the fourth-highest of the season.

While the Dragons' equipment was still in transit, the decision was made to start the game. For the first period, the Dragons wore their black practice sweaters and used the Moose's sticks, giving the contest an almost slapstick feel.

It reminded me of a time many years earlier when, as a young child, my parents took me to a small community rink to watch a junior game. Before the start of the contest, there was an adult senior league game taking place where a visiting team from nearby Pilot Mound was suited up in black longjohns. My parents and I laughed heartily at the comical scene, and I had the same reaction while watching the Dragons that night.

I would not purchase my first camera until a couple of years later, and despite the thousands of pictures that I would take during Moose games, that would be the one game I would have wanted shots from above all others.

The Dragons' equipment arrived in time for the second period, but they need not have bothered shipping it at all. The visitors offered little resistance in either of the pair of games, and the Moose coasted to easy victories. The Moose wound up the season by feasting on the league's weak sisters to sew up seventh place in the nine-team Western Conference and a date with Chicago in the first round of the playoffs.

In another nondescript *Slap Shot*-style awards ceremony before the regular-season finale, Scott Arniel was named the MVP and Brett Hauer took home the award for the best defenseman, while Brian Chapman was named the team's unsung hero. Chapman had, in fact, been the Moose's best defenseman, but Hauer's higher point total gave him the edge. It was a sad fact of life in the hockey world that defensemen were being increasingly evaluated on their offensive output rather than what they had done in their own end of the rink.

In their postseason debut, shaky goaltending doomed the Moose in both games in Chicago. Faced with a choice between two struggling netminders, Randy Carlyle opted to start Hedberg in the opener before turning to Brathwaite in the second game.

For their first playoff game in Winnipeg, the Moose unveiled their "Ignite the White" promotion, a takeoff of the White Out that had become popular during the Jets years. The White Out was a revered playoff tradition in which the fans came wearing white and cheered themselves hoarse. The tradition would be copied in other NHL cities, but none could match the level of enthusiasm of the Winnipeg White Out.

Unfortunately, the screaming white-clad crowds failed to inspire the Jets to any success. Over the course of the White Out's decade-long history, the Jets won only two series and never advanced beyond the second round. It would be no different where the Moose were concerned.

Before the Moose began play last season, Steve's brother John had jokingly suggested that the Moose should use a Brown Out instead to match the color of a real moose. It might have actually served the Moose better than a White Out.

In their home playoff debut, a surprisingly enthusiastic crowd of 7,670 turned out to see the Moose put on a display of offensive ineptitude that reached historic proportions.

"Time and time again, the Moose had glorious scoring opportunities, as Wolves goaltender Wendell Young spent most of the evening flat on his back, but the Moose would either shoot it right into Young, off the goal post, or the puck would dribble off their sticks. The third period was particularly frustrating for Moose fans, as, with the season on the line, the Moose couldn't put the puck in the ocean from the end of the pier,"[10] were my comments after the painful 1-0 loss that ended the Moose's second season. "A team with any finish around the net would have scored six or seven goals on this night easily."

"It was disappointing for the city and us to be knocked out, but we showed that we were a serious team and that our owners are serious about putting a good product on the ice,"[25] said defenseman Michael Stewart.

The atmosphere around the team was certainly much less toxic than it had been under Jean Perron, but the results were not much better. They had secured their postseason berth almost by default and were promptly swept out of the first round.

"We were able to compete, but we weren't able to win,"[26] said Carlyle.

More alarming than the lack of success on the ice, however, was the huge drop in attendance as the Moose played in front of sparse, morgue-like crowds all season long. Next year, the Moose would win much more often, but it would not bring them any closer to the Turner Cup, nor would their newfound success generate any more interest in the team.

1998-1999: False Dawn

For the first time since coming to Winnipeg, the Moose would not face the daunting task of having to build their team from scratch. Many players from last year's squad would return and the annual exodus of IHL players for Germany would cost the Moose only fighter Craig Martin.

Among the returnees were defensemen Brian Chapman, Brett Hauer, Jeff Parrott, Mike Ruark and Michael Stewart along with forwards Scott Arniel, Bill Bowler, Jimmy Roy and Scott Thomas. Ralph Intranuovo held out for an NHL opportunity that never came, and he would re-sign with the Moose midway through training camp.

To go along with the many holdovers, the Moose added a number of new players including goaltenders Christian Bronsard and Robb Stauber; defenseman Justin Kurtz; and forwards Neil Brady, Cory Cyrenne, Rhett Gordon, Jason MacDonald and Patrice Tardif.

The Moose curiously parted ways with Fred Brathwaite, who had been a fixture in the Moose goal over the past two seasons. Instead, they made the fateful decision to cast their lot with Stauber after being unable to bring Johan Hedberg back. Stauber was a seven-year veteran who had spent time in the NHL with the Los Angeles Kings and Buffalo Sabres.

The decision to go with Stauber would cost them dearly this season.

Bronsard, meanwhile, was a rookie with no pro experience. He would hold up admirably well in his infrequent appearances, but he would be relegated to the role of an inexpensive backup.

Coming off his first pro season, Kurtz attracted the Moose's interest largely because he was a Winnipeg native. He would make a modest contribution in a reserve role, but it would mostly be his birth certificate that would keep him with the Moose for the next five years.

Kurtz was drafted by the Jets three years earlier, but he turned down their contract offer because the signing bonus was "iffy."[1] It is a decision he would live to regret as he would not attract any further NHL interest for many years.

Tardif was easily the most well-known of the new Moose players, having once been part of a package of players traded for Wayne Gretzky, unquestionably the greatest star in the history of the game. I would soon discover, like virtually everyone else who had suited up for the Moose, why he had been languishing in the minor leagues.

Brady, Gordon and MacDonald were all grinders, more known for their work in the corners and along the boards than for lighting up scoreboards.

"I'm going to play my game, which is finishing my checks and playing hard,"[2] said MacDonald about his playing style.

This would be a theme that would define this season's edition of the Moose – abrasive, physical and difficult to play against. It would take them to unprecedented heights in the standings, but leave them coming up well short when matched against skilled teams. Later this season, I would use the term "drowning in grit" to describe the team's makeup.

Another Winnipeg native, Cyrenne would easily become the most infamous of the Moose's off-season additions. A rookie fresh out of the junior ranks, where he had starred with the Brandon Wheat Kings, Cyrenne signed a two-year deal with the Moose. Like Kurtz, he would parlay his birth certificate into a regular job.

Kurtz, however, would at least earn a spot on the roster. Cyrenne would do next to nothing for the Moose, becoming little more than window dressing in an unofficial affirmative action program designed to keep as many Manitobans as possible on the team.

Because of his Manitoba heritage, Cyrenne would indeed become popular with the few supporters the Moose had. Desperate to retain every last customer, the Moose undoubtedly felt compelled to keep him on the team for that reason. However, if Chipman and Carlyle had studied their history and knew more about Winnipeg hockey fans, they would have realized that replacing Cyrenne with a productive player may have instead improved the team's bottom line.

Decades earlier, Jets founder Ben Hatskin had stocked the team's inaugural roster with Manitobans in order to appeal to local fans. Despite their success, however, the Jets had tremendous difficulty drawing crowds in those early years. It was not until the arrival of the Swedes two years later that a Jets ticket became a hot commodity. The Swedish players turned a dull, plodding squad into the most exciting, fast-skating team in the game, and the fans responded accordingly by packing the rink.

Soon after the Jets had entered the NHL, general manager John Ferguson made an unpopular trade when he sent Willy Lindstrom to Edmonton in exchange for Laurie Boschman. An integral part of all three AVCO Cup championship teams with the Jets, Lindstrom had been a fan favorite for many years. Boschman, meanwhile, was a former first-round draft choice whose career appeared to be going nowhere.

Ferguson took a lot of heat for the deal, but Boschman would quickly develop into a cornerstone player for the Jets for many years to come. Fans warmed to Boschman just as quickly, and they soon forgot about Willy Lindstrom.

Like fans in other cities, Winnipeggers wanted to see good hockey players. They appreciated a quality product and had proven their willingness over the years to support it regardless of where the players were born. Players who produced became fan favorites. Those who didn't were booed lustily.

For the second time in as many seasons, Greg Pankewicz tried out with the Calgary Flames, but this time, he would make their opening-night roster. However, he would do little in his brief fling with the Flames and would spend most of the season with their farm team in Saint John. He would eventually find his way back to the IHL, where the Moose would have to deal with him as an opponent.

In addition to Pankewicz, the Moose also lost Brad Purdie, their second-leading scorer last season, to the Fort Wayne Komets.

Around the league, the IHL lost two more teams when the San Antonio Dragons and Quebec Rafales closed up shop, leaving the league with 16 franchises. Longtime commissioner Bob Ufer resigned and was replaced by former Sabres president Doug Moss. It would be Moss who would steer the IHL away from its path of being a second-tier NHL competitor, but little could he have known that he was several years too late to save the venerable old league. He would instead go down in history as the IHL's last commissioner.

The league lost another NHL affiliation when the Islanders pulled out of Utah, leaving the Grizzlies as an independent team. The Nashville Predators, however, decided to hook up with Milwaukee and use the Admirals as the expansion franchise's first farm team.

The Moose remained an independent team, but not for lack of effort on Chipman's part to consummate a partial affiliation agreement with the Edmonton Oilers. That Chipman would even *consider* such an arrangement made my blood run cold.

During their nearly two decades in the NHL, the Jets had become the Oilers' favorite whipping boys. Rarely did Edmonton as much as have to break a sweat to beat their division rivals. At one point, they had run up a 20-game winning streak over the Jets in regular-season play and another 16-game streak in playoff competition.

What made those endless defeats more painful was how passive and meek the Jets played against Edmonton. They were often so paralyzed by their own fear of the vaunted Oilers that they were as good as beaten before ever stepping onto the ice.

To many lifelong Jets fans like me, the Oilers became the living embodiment of the Evil Empire that threatened the planet with a nuclear holocaust. Snuggling up with the Oilers would have been sacrilege of the highest order. Treason, in fact. And if Chipman had the audacity to pull off an affiliation with them, I would have instantly ceased to be a fan of the Moose.

Chipman continued his dialogue with the Oilers into the season, but fortunately, this unholy alliance never came to pass, and for better or for worse, I continued to follow the Moose.

The same could not be said for many other Winnipeg hockey fans. The Moose remained as well accepted as a loaf of day-old bread and financial losses from last season were expected to top $1 million. Chipman, however, became convinced that the solution to the Moose's problems was building a new arena, rather than trying to attract more customers to the Moose's current home rink.

The Winnipeg Arena was indeed a dump. Though structurally sound, it was not well maintained and a haven for vermin. That said, in spite of its shortcomings, it was hardly a factor in keeping fans away from Moose games. There was ample seating and good sight lines, and the facility was conveniently located, with plenty of unofficial free parking at an adjacent shopping mall.

With the involuntary assistance of Manitoba taxpayers, Chipman would eventually get his arena, but it would have more fans than the team itself.

The only drama from training camp came when Jason MacDonald's van full of his personal belongings was stolen from a parking lot near the Arena. The van was later recovered, but without his belongings and the van's tires. MacDonald became but one in a long list of victims to learn the hard way that Winnipeg was the auto theft capital of North America.

In their exhibition schedule, the Moose won two and tied one of three games against the Canadian national team before taking two of three over IHL opponents.

Capitalizing on some weak goaltending, the Moose opened the regular season with a pair of victories in Orlando. With five points over the two games, Scott Thomas was named the IHL's Player of the Week.

Back home, the Moose laid an egg in a 6-2 blowout defeat at the hands of the Long Beach Ice Dogs. The surprisingly good crowd of 8,500 began booing in the second period, and after falling behind, the Moose "seemed more concerned with fighting than with attempting a comeback,"[3] as I wrote after the game. For the first time since moving to Winnipeg, however, the Moose at least scored a goal in their home opener.

Before the game, the Moose observed a moment of silence in honor of Stephane Morin, who had recently died of heart failure during a German league game. While playing for the Berlin Capitals, the former Moose star collapsed at the bench five minutes into the second period and was eventually pronounced dead after attempts to revive him had failed.

Over the weekend, in a classy gesture, the Moose wives raised $2,000 for Morin's family with a game-worn jersey raffle.

Naturally, I had posted the news of Morin's tragic death on the front page of my Moose site. Fiona Quick would later send me an e-mail strongly urging me to put Morin's name in black instead of the purple that I used on the rest of the site to match the predominant color in the Moose logo. I found those instructions odd coming from someone who was easily his most vocal critic in cyberspace.

The Moose split their next two games before embarking on a unique "Made in the IHL" scheduling odyssey that would see them play four consecutive games against the Indianapolis Ice. Playing next door to an alpaca and llama exhibition, the Moose edged the Ice 3-2 at the Pepsi Coliseum to take the opener.

Pepsi Coliseum.[5]

After playing at the more modern Market Square Arena, the Ice had moved back to the Pepsi Coliseum at the Indiana State Fairgrounds this season. Supposedly refurbished, the Coliseum remained a rat hole, but economics was the driving force behind the move as the team saved $8,000 per game in rent over what they had been paying at Market Square Arena.

The next two games took place in Winnipeg, where sparse crowds saw each team win once. Robb Stauber's porous goaltending and an embarrassing late giveaway by Brett Hauer sent the Moose down in the first of the two, but they rebounded to post a 7-4 win on Halloween two nights later. In pregame promotions, the Moose had promised a "scary" evening for Halloween, but as I wrote, "the only thing scary was the lack of paying customers in the building."[3] The announced attendance was only 4,105, officially their second-lowest crowd since moving to Winnipeg.

There would be many more even smaller crowds to come in future years, but official figures would not come close to reflecting the actual number of people in the stands. Through Rob Gialloreto, the Moose denied falsifying attendance numbers, but the gap between the announced attendance and the actual head count in the building would grow steadily. However the Moose justified their official numbers, be it through freebies or special promotions, those two figures just weren't matching.

The announcement of the attendance would eventually become just as entertaining as the game itself. There were times when I would nearly laugh out loud on the bus when I heard Kelly Moore giving the official crowd count on the radio.

This weekend also featured the debut of "Moose News," a *Free Press* supplement with various articles on the team written by Moose staffers that would appear every other week. Oddly, rather than being part of the sports section, it would be instead inserted into the color comics. This would be one of many reasons why the team was never taken seriously.

Before the return engagement in Indianapolis, Stauber stunned the Moose by suddenly announcing his retirement.

"Throughout the summer, I could feel the fire starting to slip away but I felt I owed it to myself to come back and really put my best foot forward. I did and it wasn't there for a lot of reasons,"[4] said Stauber.

Stauber's performance was anything but stellar through the first month of the season, but his untimely retirement left the Moose in the lurch scrambling for a goaltender. Fortunately, they quickly found one in 27-year-old Richard Shulmistra.

Shulmistra was a New Jersey Devils prospect who was one of three goaltenders with their farm team in Albany. Initially assigned to the Moose on a two-week loan, the two teams would quickly work out a longer-term arrangement for Shulmistra to stay in Winnipeg.

Tall and imposing in the net and solid as a rock night after night, Shulmistra would become a godsend for the Moose. Johan Hedberg would later achieve much more notoriety, but Shulmistra would, in fact, become the best goaltender the Moose would have during their years in the IHL. At times, he would stand so far above his contemporaries that he looked like a man among boys. A bright future seemed a virtual certainty for him, yet to my immense surprise, he was never able to establish himself as a regular in the NHL.

Nonetheless, Shulmistra's spectacular goaltending appeared to be the final piece of the puzzle to make the Moose a legitimate contender for the Turner Cup, or so it seemed. Regrettably, the clock would strike midnight prematurely, giving this Cinderella story an unhappy ending.

Of the many needs the Moose addressed during the summer, there was one glaring omission – a fighter. They would address that need in spades the following day with the acquisition of 6-foot-4, 225-pound Jason Shmyr.

Shmyr had started the season with Long Beach, but he was dropped from the roster and was working out with the San Diego Gulls of the West Coast Hockey League when the Moose called.

"He's been able to defend his teammates and stand up for his teammates. He fits the role we've been searching for for a long time,"[5] said Carlyle.

Jason Shmyr.[1]

Shmyr would not only defend his teammates, but also put the fear of God into players around the league.

He was slow as a boat anchor, but there was no tougher hombre in the game at any level. Anyone who dared take any liberties with his teammates faced the wrath of a coldly efficient professional pugilist. Expressionless and stone-faced, he would use his fists like battering rams to pound his opponents into absolute submission.

"I never look at who I have to impress in the crowd. It's my teammates that I have to protect,"[6] said Shmyr.

But impress he did. By the end of the season, Shmyr would establish himself as one of the most legendary figures in Moose history. Next season, I would name my unofficial award for the most fighting majors in a season in his honor and feature the standings for the

"Jason Shmyr Award" prominently on the front page of my Moose site.

With their new additions in the lineup, the Moose went on a bit of a roll while dealing with a firestorm of media attention surrounding another new signee, 29-year-old Brandon, Manitoba native Sheldon Kennedy.

Out of the game since breaking his leg more than a year ago, the veteran of eight nondescript NHL seasons was far more noted for being the victim of sexual abuse at the hands of his former coach, Graham James. After Kennedy went public with his story, James was subsequently convicted of two counts of sexual assault and sentenced to three and a half years in jail.

"All we're trying to do is provide an opportunity for Sheldon Kennedy to get his career back on track,"[7] said Carlyle.

Among the new faces in Chicago's lineup as they made their first appearance of the season at the Arena was former Jet Ed Olczyk. Olczyk would be just one of a parade of prominent former Jets including Stephane Beauregard, Tim Cheveldae, Kris King, Jim Kyte, Troy Murray, Pat Elynuik and Nikolai Khabibulin who would come in with a visiting team to face the Moose.

Olczyk, like many of his former teammates, would receive only a smattering of polite applause upon his introduction. It was as if those former Jets had never even played in Winnipeg, almost like there had been no Winnipeg Jets at all.

Chipman would claim that 75% of his subscribers were former Jets season ticket holders. The tepid reaction from the crowd to the former Jets would strongly rebut that allegation.

After working his way back into shape, Kennedy made his much-anticipated debut and scored the winning goal as the Moose beat the Blades 5-2. Everything seemed to click for the Moose that night except for the printers at the box office.

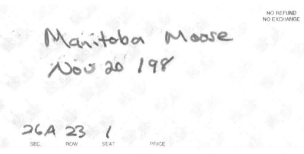

Handwritten ticket stub from November 20, 1998.[9]

When I walked up to the ticket window and asked for my seat, the Select-A-Seat clerk took out a blank ticket and wrote the game date and seat number on it with a black felt-tip marker.

"Don't worry, it'll work," he said as I stared down at the handwritten ticket in disbelief. To my surprise, the ticket taker didn't flinch when I handed him the ticket and passed through the front doors.

Backstopped by Shulmistra and powered by some timely contributions up and down the roster, the Moose rattled off a 13-game unbeaten streak. Even without Brian Chapman, their defensive bulwark, who was serving a five-game suspension for using his stick like a razor blade to cut Dennis Vial for 25 stitches, the Moose barely missed a beat. They even found a way to beat their nemesis, Chicago's Wendell Young.

"We think we can match up against any team in this league,"[8] crowed Bill Bowler.

The red-hot Moose cooled off slightly, but they still were only three points out of first place as they prepared to host the Las Vegas

Thunder for a pair of weekend games in the last week before Christmas.

In Friday's opener, former Jet and Moose Russ Romaniuk scored twice and the league's worst team got the better of the Moose in the shootout to take a 4-3 win. The Moose rebounded to take Sunday afternoon's finale 4-2 over a team so ravaged by injuries that they had to suit up amateur player Ray Clarke. Clarke was the second player in as many years from the HTHL to suit up in a Moose game at the Arena, and unlike emergency goaltender Bob Brisebois last year, Clarke actually saw game action.

The final score, however, took a back seat to the melee that took place in the game's dying seconds following a faceoff in the Moose zone. Jason Shmyr got things going by giving Shawn Wansborough a facewash, and seconds later, the donnybrook was in full swing once Thunder goaltender Scott Langkow skated the length of the ice to join the action. Even after being ushered to the penalty box, Shmyr tried to scale the glass to get at Thunder defenseman Sami Helenius.

While the fists were flying on the ice, over at the Thunder bench, coach Bob Bourne took a stick and banged it on the glass in the direction of a fan who had been giving him a hard time all afternoon long.

As the officials tried desperately to regain control and steer the combatants to their respective dressing rooms, Chipman noticed that his counterpart, Thunder general manager Bob Strumm, was trying to stop his players from leaving the ice. Strumm would later say he was just trying to make sure his team was not undermanned, since many Moose players were still on the ice and tempers were still raging.

After the brawl was over, Chipman made the mistake of going down to ice level to confront Strumm right in front of the Thunder dressing room.

Bob Strumm was a heavyset, balding, highfalutin swashbuckler who strutted around like a rooster that ruled the hen house. Chipman should have known that Strumm was the last person in the building who was going to take any guff from him or anyone else. Not surprisingly, in no uncertain terms, Strumm promptly invited his opposite number to leave.

"I don't know what Mark's problem is. He's obviously upset about the events at the end of the game that his player has admitted starting. As usual, he's trying to deflect blame on somebody else," said Strumm. "It always seems like Winnipeg is so pure and Mark is this purified representative of hockey and they're never at fault."[9]

Shmyr would later serve a two-game suspension for his role in the fracas and be fined $150.

Following an arduous seven-game, two-week road trip, the Moose got back on the winning track with a sweep of the Grizzlies in a pair of weekend games back at the Arena.

Before taking on the Solar Bears for a pair the following weekend, the Moose announced that Sheldon Kennedy was leaving to join EV Landshut in Germany.

"As it was presented to us, going to play in Europe is the best situation for Sheldon Kennedy and his family. In this instance, we allowed Sheldon to pursue this step in his hockey career,"[10] said Carlyle.

I would come to have great compassion for all that Kennedy had suffered, but I deeply resented his decision to quit the team in the middle of the season. As with any other Moose player, I would have been thrilled for him if he had an opportunity to get back to the NHL, but to make what amounted to a lateral move left a bad taste in my mouth. I hope there were extenuating circumstances that justified his premature departure.

As the Moose remained among the Western Conference leaders, Chipman rewarded Carlyle with a two-year contract extension in early February.

"The people I'm involved with here are committed to making this thing go. This is all part of it,"[11] said Carlyle. That commitment would leave much to be desired.

The Moose began to catch fire again and took a pair from the league-leading Aeros as part of another long unbeaten streak. They lost their next three before a 3-2 come-from-behind victory over the Vipers on a Sunday afternoon at the Arena, winning only their fourth of 13 shootout decisions so far this season.

Among the four fights that afternoon was a first-period battle between Patrice Tardif and John Emmons of the Vipers. While Keith Aldridge and Ralph Intranuovo were engaged in a battle of their own, Emmons goaded Tardif into a fight. Since any player involved in a fight after the original altercation is automatically ejected, it was a clever bit of gamesmanship by Emmons to take Tardif, one of the Moose's best players, out of the game.

Though this would be the only occasion in which Tardif would actually be thrown out of a game while with the Moose, he would fall victim to this ploy many other times. Opponents across the league would regularly sucker him into taking needless penalties just to get him off the ice.

Tardif was tall with good size, but he was anything but a fighter or scrapper. Unfortunately, he was also not the smartest player the Moose ever had, and he would exhibit the most eccentric and bizarre behavior of any player to ever suit up for the Moose.

He was always fidgety and anxious, seemingly unable to stay still, even during stoppages, yet there was such a pained weariness etched on his face that it looked like he had been awake for a month. His eyes were as wide as flying saucers, and they looked like they were about to pop out of their sockets. My friend Steve quickly branded him with the derisive nickname "Buggy Eyes."

In the faceoff circle, he would endlessly roll his stick in his hands and always put his stick down before his opponent, even though players on the home team had the advantage of being able to put their stick down last.

I always thought of Tardif when I read stories about former players who had fallen on hard times and were now living out of the back seat of their car or in a homeless shelter. Without a doubt, he would be the one Moose player voted most likely to be among that group.

Tardif had immense skills, and it was easy to see why he had been included in a trade for Wayne Gretzky, but he just didn't have the hockey sense to make it in the NHL. In baseball parlance, there's a common expression about such a player. Million-dollar arm. Fifty-cent head.

The Moose won all four games of a road trip before returning to host Kansas City for a pair of weekend games. For Saturday night's finale, I walked up to the box office and asked for my regular seat. I was blown away when the clerk told me that nothing in that entire section was available.

"All sold," he said.

What gives? Had Moose hockey suddenly become a hot ticket?

I felt oddly fortunate that he found me an unsold single seat on the opposite side of the ice, and I sat down expecting to be part of an overflow crowd. Instead, it was yet another paltry gathering that snoozed through a poor effort by the Moose, who lost for the second time in as many nights.

While the Moose spent the night mouthing off at referee Todd Anderson, I could not take my eyes off the vast tracts of empty seats and, in some cases, entire sections. In the section I had been specifically told was completely sold out, there were not more than a handful of randomly scattered spectators.

The announced attendance was 10,563, but there were likely no more than half that number actually in the building. Early the following week, I would learn that the Moose had put together a deal where they had turned over nearly all of their remaining unsold tickets to Pizza Hut for them to give to their customers. For all I knew, Moose tickets were being shoved inside pizza boxes and delivery customers were using them like napkins to wipe their faces after polishing off a 16-inch supreme with double cheese. These so-called sellouts were more likely "giveouts."

When I queried him about it, Rob Gialloreto vehemently denied that the Moose were giving away free tickets en masse and seemed quite offended by the suggestion that these sellouts were something less than legitimate. The Moose were undoubtedly receiving some financial considerations in the deal, but in all probability, this was a case of unloading excess inventory at fire-sale prices.

The Moose continued their winning ways and kept the heat on the first-place Wolves. Even fighter Jason Shmyr chipped in with an assist, putting him only one point behind each of the two goaltenders.

With the start of the playoffs just around the corner, amid a swirl of controversy, the Devils recalled Richard Shulmistra and re-assigned him to their farm team in Albany for the remainder of the year. Publicly, the Devils claimed their regular goaltender in Albany had become seriously ill, but the impetus for the move may have actually come from Shulmistra.

Soon after Shulmistra's departure, Ashley Prest and Tim Campbell of the *Free Press* wrote, "While with the Moose, the 27-year-old goalie [Shulmistra] never made a secret he preferred being with a top NHL farm team, something he confirmed this week."[12]

In any event, for the second time this season, the Moose were left to scramble for a goaltender. Their first choice was NHL veteran Corey Hirsch, but even though Hirsch was more than agreeable, various technicalities prevented his assignment. They were forced to settle for 31-year-old Mike Rosati, who had spent most of his pro career split between stints in Italy and Germany. This season, he had been floundering on a bad team in Portland and welcomed the chance to play for a contender.

Rosati performed well in his first appearances in a Moose uniform, but the Moose were unable to keep pace with Chicago, leaving them relegated to second place.

As the regular season wound down, Shmyr took on a starring role. On a Wednesday night against Milwaukee, Shmyr threw a vicious elbow that sent Admirals defenseman Richard Lintner staggering off the ice with a concussion. In the finale, he took a regular shift and was named the game's first star after scoring his only goal of the season.

Though he was primarily on the team to fight, Shmyr had actually seen time on the Moose's top line alongside Bill Bowler and Scott Thomas. He was no slower than the aging Scott Arniel, who normally occupied that spot, and Shmyr's physical presence would create a lot more room for the two slick skaters.

The Moose began the playoffs with a best-of-three preliminary-round series against the Admirals. Despite being outplayed, the Moose took the opener in Milwaukee before returning to Winnipeg for Game 2, where the two teams staged an epic battle. The Moose fought back from an early deficit, and Bowler's goal midway through the second overtime gave the Moose their first-ever series victory.

The dramatic win would easily stand as the biggest in franchise history. Sadly, it would be the Moose's last win of the season.

The Moose were still in good spirits as they prepared for their next challenge, a best-of-five series against the hated Wolves.

"Confidence is the biggest thing we have right now,"[13] said Brett Hauer.

Unfortunately, it would not last long.

After dropping a hard-fought 2-1 decision in Chicago in the series opener, the Moose battled the Wolves on even terms through regulation two nights later, only to lose on a long, weak shot in overtime that eluded Rosati. Back at the Arena for Game 3, a legitimate near-sellout crowd saw the Moose go down meekly to bring their season to an end. As he had been throughout much of the playoffs, Rosati was again porous and was replaced by Christian Bronsard to start the third period.

Moose captain Scott Arniel opened the scoring, netting what would be his last goal as a pro. After the game, fighting back tears, he announced his retirement as a player. A consummate team player, Arniel had a long and memorable playing career that began with the Jets nearly two decades earlier. This year, however, had been a struggle for "Captain Fantastic," as Kelly Moore dubbed him. His speed had deserted him, and he was often so far behind the play that, at times, he became a liability on the ice. His was the case of a player who had retired one year too late.

On the ice, despite their swift exit from the playoffs, the Moose had an outstanding season. Their 47-21-14 record placed them fourth overall in the league, and they were in contention for the top spot in the Midwest Division for most of the year. They placed four players in the midseason All-Star Game and three more on the postseason all-league teams.

Like their artificially inflated attendance numbers, however, it would all prove to be a mirage.

"It's a tribute to what Mark [Chipman] and his staff have done in Winnipeg. Those people have made the Manitoba Moose one of the league's real success stories,"[14] said IHL commissioner Doug Moss.

If this was the IHL's definition of a success story, it was no wonder the league would have only two years to live.

1999-2000: Crash Landing

Fresh off their best season ever, expectations were running at a fever pitch as the Moose embarked on their fourth season in Manitoba.

"Our hockey club is ready to take the next step – our goal is the Turner Cup,"[1] said Randy Carlyle.

Sadly, that next step would be backwards.

The Moose were able to bring back a number of players from their record-setting season a year ago. Returning were team MVP Bill Bowler; defensemen Brian Chapman, Justin Kurtz, Jeff Parrott, Mike Ruark and Michael Stewart; and forwards Jason MacDonald and Patrice Tardif.

Brett Hauer at last looked like he would get a bona fide chance to crack an NHL roster when the Tampa Bay Lightning signed him to an offer sheet. Once again, however, the Edmonton Oilers, who had no interest in his services, inexplicably exercised their right to match the offer, thus blocking what was, in reality, his last and best shot at moving up. The Oilers held Hauer in such disregard that they would not even invite him to training camp and instead simply assigned him back to the Moose.

"It's sad. My NHL window is getting smaller. I'm getting older. I just wanted another fair chance,"[2] said a despondent Hauer.

Hauer was a man who wore his heart on his sleeve each and every night. No player gave more effort and tried harder. He was prone to the odd untimely defensive lapse, but he was nonetheless a fluid and graceful skater and an offensively gifted playmaker. The mirror opposite of Brian Chapman, he probably never threw a bodycheck or as much as cast a disparaging look at an opponent during his four years in a Moose uniform. Nonetheless, he was a great asset to the team. I was thrilled to have him back, but I felt so bad for him personally.

Most players at this level had either seen their big chance come and go or never did earn that chance. On the heels of what had been an outstanding season, Hauer had clearly earned his NHL opportunity, yet the Oilers again stood in his way, seemingly almost with malice. His case was perhaps the most tragic of all during the Moose's years in the IHL.

Hauer would instead have to settle for being what in baseball parlance is called a "AAAA" player, one who was too good to be in the minors, yet apparently not good enough to warrant a shot at the big leagues. To his credit, however, though he was obviously and rightly bitter towards the Oilers, he would never let it affect his play with the Moose, and he would again enjoy a fine season.

Not that I needed one, but Hauer's situation gave me yet another reason to hate the Oilers. It also made me even more resentful of Mark Chipman's efforts to have the Moose become an Oilers affiliate.

One player who did get an NHL opportunity was Scott Thomas, the Moose's leading goal scorer a year ago, who signed with the Los Angeles Kings. In addition, fighter Jason Shmyr signed with the Washington Capitals organization. The annual migration of IHL players to Germany cost the Moose only winger Ralph Intranuovo and defenseman Kent Fearns.

New signings this year would include tiny centerman Eric Veilleux, minor-league journeyman winger Mike Prokopec and centerman Lonny Bohonos. A Winnipeg native, Bohonos was the Moose's marquee off-season acquisition for reasons other than his Manitoba birth certificate. He was a veteran with 83 NHL games to his credit who had played a starring role with the Toronto Maple Leafs in the Stanley Cup playoffs this past season.

The addition of Bohonos, however, would not quite be the panacea the Moose had envisioned. Like many other high-profile players the Moose had and would bring in, fans would soon learn why he had not been able to stick with an NHL team.

Though unable to strike a deal with the Oilers, the Moose did work out an unofficial partial affiliation agreement with the Detroit Red Wings. That affiliation would net them three players: forward Marc Rodgers and goaltenders Jason Elliott and Manny Legace. Each would become major contributors this year.

Rodgers was a minor-league veteran known as more of a grinder, while Elliott was coming off a fine rookie pro season. A rising prospect, Legace would be the big prize in this unofficial affiliation, but he would not be able to join the Moose until late October, leaving Elliott to carry the load for the early part of the season.

Off the ice, following his overdue retirement as a player, Scott Arniel would move behind the bench to assist Carlyle, while Craig Heisinger made the curious transition from equipment manager to assistant general manager.

For the first time since moving to Winnipeg, the Moose would not appear on local television this season. My only source for the Moose on television this year would be my C-band satellite dish.

Around the league, the Fort Wayne Komets, one of the league's oldest and most venerable franchises, folded along with the Las Vegas Thunder. The remaining 13 teams were realigned into two conferences with the affiliated teams in the east and the independent clubs in the west.

Since I had been going to so many games over the past three years, I decided to buy a mini-pack to take advantage of the $3-per-game discount. I made my first and only trip to the Moose offices on September 2 and after interrupting the receptionist's beauty sleep, I stepped into the office of account executive Kristy Nykoluk.

Expecting someone as indifferent as a game-day usher, I was a little caught off guard when the young and flighty Kristy pounced on me like a buzzard who had just spotted some fresh roadkill. It was obvious I was her first and likely only customer of the day.

I promptly selected my seat and chose 21 of the 41 games in the home schedule. Kristy ran my credit card through and I became a registered "stakeholder."

For the mini-pack that I would hold for the next three years, I selected section 26, row 18, seat 1. Nestled high up against a wall in the southeast corner, it was a seat I had been purchasing regularly over the past couple of seasons. It offered a good panoramic view of the ice while being far enough away from the action to avoid most of the hordes of children that roamed freely throughout the stands.

Section 26, to the immediate left of the video board.[1]

For the most part, the strategy paid off as I was allowed to enjoy the games in relative peace more often than in any other seat in the

Arena. The children, however, would eventually find me and do their part to make my game-night experience miserable. Some adults, too, would also make their way there and prove just as obnoxious as the children.

On one particular night, I had gone to the washroom during the first intermission only to return and find two older gentlemen sprawled out next to my seat. They had moved from another section, and despite the presence of so many empty sections in the area, they spent the rest of the night snuggled up next to me. Even after getting up to go to the washroom in the next intermission, they came back and again dropped anchor in those seats to my right.

On principle, I refused to move. This was the seat I had paid for, and I was not going to leave to accommodate their claim to squatter's rights.

After the game was over and the three stars were announced, rather than turn and exit via the opposite end of the row that was completely unoccupied, they tried to push their way past me. They became visibly annoyed as I blocked their path and kept them waiting for several minutes. What was good for the goose was also good for the gander.

The day after I had purchased my mini-pack, Winnipeg mayor Glen Murray officially kicked off the Moose's season ticket campaign. As one of the team's few devoted followers, I did not know the Moose even had a season ticket campaign until many years later when I uncovered this detail in the *Free Press* archives while doing research for this book.

Following a week-long training camp at the Highlander Sportsplex, the Moose began their exhibition schedule with a three-game sweep of the Canadian national team. The Moose then racked up a dozen fights while taking two of three games from IHL opponents. Brian

Chapman was named the new captain and would carry that position with distinction for the next four years, up until the time of his unceremonious release.

"We as an organization and our coaching staff have put higher expectations on our season. Hopefully that translates into more success,"[3] said Carlyle on the eve of the league opener on Friday, October 1, against Chicago.

Not surprisingly, it wouldn't.

The Moose opened the season on a high note with a pair of victories over the weekend. In Sunday afternoon's win over Kansas City, Jimmy Roy began what would become a particularly vicious season-long blood feud between the two clubs when he bowled over Dody Wood from behind late in the second period. Watching Roy's back was fighter Larry Shapley, who was making his Moose debut after being acquired on loan from the Vancouver Canucks organization.

Shapley was a 21-year-old, 6-foot-6 behemoth of a man who could barely stand up on skates. It looked like he could have moved faster if he had been able to swap his skates for a pair of rubber boots. From a distance, he looked like a giant toy soldier that Carlyle would wind up from behind and push in the general direction of the opponent's fighter. No one was bigger or tougher than Larry Shapley, but he was utterly devoid of hockey skills and would undoubtedly have been better served to ply his trade in a boxing ring.

"The guy was a monster and truly defined the word GOON, he could do nothing else,"[4] recalled a poster on hockey-fights.com who had seen him play in junior hockey.

Shapley would not last long with the Moose, and his pro hockey career would end after a brief stint in the ECHL later in the year.

Before taking off to begin their first road trip of the year, the Moose picked up 26-year-old winger Jim Campbell on loan from the St. Louis Blues. Plagued by stomach muscle and groin tears last year, Campbell was trying to get his career back on track following surgery in April.

Instead of making an effort to impress, however, Campbell would do little but sulk during his brief stay with the Moose. He would quickly find his way into Carlyle's doghouse before being returned to St. Louis.

"We didn't like the way he played there," said Blues general manager Larry Pleau. "We watched him play six or seven games and he wasn't working very hard."[4]

The case of a player moping over an assignment to the minor leagues was generally more common in the AHL than in the IHL. By and large, most players in the IHL knew their chance at stardom had come and gone and had long since been resigned to their fate. In the AHL, a league stocked with young players fresh from the junior ranks, it was very different. Big-league dreams were still burning brightly, and being exiled to the minors was seen as an embarrassment.

Following a lackluster 5-2 defeat in Detroit, the Moose's never-ending woes in the shootout continued in a 3-2 loss to Orlando. Mike Prokopec was the only one of seven Moose shooters who scored in the penalty-shot contest. Sadly, he would soon fall in line with the rest of his new teammates and would score only once more in his next 11 shootout attempts during the rest of the year.

Prokopec was a big, lumbering winger who scored most of his goals banging and crashing in front of the net. He had no slick moves in his repertoire and not much of a scoring touch. Aside from Shapley and the two goaltenders, he was probably the one player on the roster least likely to score in a shootout. To coin one of my father's favorite phrases, he couldn't shoot his way out of a wet paper bag.

Time and again, however, Carlyle would bullheadedly keep sending Prokopec over the boards in the shootout. In making Prokopec one of his first choices, it almost seemed as though Carlyle wanted to get Prokopec's miss out of the way early before he sent his more skilled players out to take their turn.

This would not be the last time Carlyle's obstinacy would take center stage. It would become a much greater issue the following year and nearly cost them a playoff berth.

The Moose wound up their first road trip of the season with a 4-2 victory in Cincinnati. Scoring once and adding an assist was 21-year-old Vladislav Serov, who earned a contract with a strong showing in training camp. The 5-foot-10 Serov would not make a big impact with the Moose, but he was brilliant at times in these early-season games and showed some real potential before his eventual demotion to the Flint Generals of the United Hockey League (UHL).

In his half-season with the Moose, however, Serov would show much more than Cory Cyrenne ever would over parts of three seasons. Yet it would be Serov who would be demoted while Cyrenne remained with the Moose. No doubt, the roles would have been reversed if Serov was the one holding a Manitoba birth certificate instead of Cyrenne.

The Moose had an up and down start to their season, and that frustrating inconsistency would linger all year long. Once again, few noticed as the Arena was rarely more than half full through the first three months of the season.

Thirty-year-old Jim Montgomery joined the Moose on loan from the Philadelphia Flyers organization and though he would be one of their top scorers this year, his efforts would do little to pull the team out of the doldrums.

The ever-struggling Cyrenne was mercifully assigned to Flint for a 14-day conditioning stint in mid-November. Cyrenne, however, refused the temporary assignment and was subsequently suspended.

"When I got there, my head and my heart just weren't into it. I wouldn't be helping the Flint Generals hockey team or myself as a hockey player,"[6] said Cyrenne.

Given his status as hockey's equivalent of a kept man, Cyrenne's refusal to report to Flint was one of the biggest acts of chutzpah in the history of the game. He was not just an unproductive player, but utterly lost and badly overmatched at this level. He reminded me of a small child separated from his mother in a crowded shopping mall on the day before Christmas.

He was not without skills and I could see how he was able to be so successful against the smaller, less experienced players in junior hockey. When facing professionals, however, he was nowhere near up to the challenge.

After spending a few days sulking, Cyrenne would eventually reconsider and report to Flint. A week later, he was back with the Moose, and the almost mystical hold he had over his employer would continue unabated, even after his forgettable playing career had ended. He would go on to work for the Moose in the front office and, later, with the Birchwood Automotive Group, the Chipman family's chain of car dealerships.

In late November, the Moose endured another in a series of gut-wrenching defeats when they dropped a 4-3 decision in Cleveland. In the game's final minute, Brett Hauer had a clear path to the net, only to pass up a glorious opportunity by dishing off to the stone-handed

Prokopec. After Prokopec failed to stuff in the equalizer, Lonny Bohonos followed by gassing an equally good chance of his own. With almost a wide-open net staring him in the face, he couldn't put the puck over the sprawling Evgeni Nabokov in the Lumberjacks goal.

That late-game miss would come to sum up his tenure with the Moose in a microcosm. Bohonos clearly had the talent to make it in the NHL, but he always seemed to come up short when the game was on the line. In addition, much like Patrice Tardif, his hockey sense would leave much to be desired.

A few weeks earlier, Bohonos had taken a page out of the playbook of his flaky teammate, who was on the shelf for a month after breaking his hand in a senseless fight. With his team trailing in the third period and badly needing their skilled players on the ice, Bohonos picked a fight with Ty Jones of the Lumberjacks. Later in the year, he would pull off another of Tardif's patented moves when he took a silly retaliation penalty in a tied game to take himself out of the subsequent shootout.

His assignment to the Moose would be anything but a triumphant homecoming. Instead, he would best be remembered by Moose fans as an enigma rather than as a good hockey player.

As was the case with their season, the Moose's rivalry with the Blades also began to spiral out of control.

Off the ice, Matt Frost, the Moose's new media relations coordinator, was reported to have said something "highly inappropriate"[7] to Blades coach and former Jet Paul MacLean after a game. A week later, the Blades retaliated by banning Kelly Moore from access to their team on the day of the game.

In that game in Kansas City, after Brendan Yarema had tried to gouge Jimmy Roy's eyes, Grant Richison and Bill Bowler were involved in a nasty stick-swinging incident. Though Bowler would later shrug off the affair with the comment "Nobody got hurt so let's move on,"[8] the league would not be quite so forgiving as both players would be suspended for two games. There was also an allegation of a confrontation between a Moose player and a fan. In their next trip, the Moose would bring security personnel of their own to investigate the incident.

IHL vice president Bob McCammon flew to Winnipeg for the rematch and read the riot act to both coaches before the game, but his words hardly dampened the raging hostilities between the two teams. Dody Wood settled an old score by driving his stick into Roy's gut in their next meeting, and many more fights would ensue in subsequent games, each one a vicious grudge match.

It was ironic that both coaches, each a former Jet, were key components of one of the NHL's most passive and meek teams. Had the Jets of that era played with anywhere close to the level of intensity their teams had showed this year, the Jets would likely have enjoyed considerably more success, thus possibly postponing or preventing their eventual departure.

Making his Moose debut in an early-December victory over the Houston Aeros was 27-year-old Rusty Fitzgerald, who was summoned from the Quad City Mallards of the UHL. Fitzgerald broke into pro hockey with the Pittsburgh Penguins, but he suffered a devastating knee injury that not only derailed his NHL aspirations but nearly ended his career. The Moose had signed him last summer, but he had still not fully recovered and was unable to attend training camp.

From the first moment he put on a Moose uniform, he looked absolutely as slow as molasses and even appeared to have trouble standing up on skates. It was obvious the injury had completely robbed him of what little speed he once had. Any playmaking skills he ever had were also long gone. This awkwardly built collection of loosely assembled body parts that was held together with spit and bailing wire had little more than guts and hard work to offer.

After first seeing him play, I didn't figure him to last more than a week with the Moose. Against all odds, however, he would become one of their most effective scorers, racking up 48 goals over the next year and a half. How he had managed to become such a sniper would be the biggest unsolved mystery in the history of the franchise. So many of his teammates, even including Cyrenne, had much more skill and finesse, yet it would be Fitzgerald who would keep lighting up the scoreboard.

Fittingly, Fitzgerald would be the last recipient of the John Cullen Award, previously known as the Comeback Player of the Year, "awarded to the player deemed to have been a key contributor to his team, while overcoming injury, illness, or other personal setbacks."

In early December, the Moose picked up 27-year-old winger Corey Spring and 25-year-old fighter Doug Doull from the Detroit Vipers. Spring would not last long with the Moose, but by the time the year was out, it would be a record-setting season for Doull. Even though he had joined the Moose midway through the year, he would eclipse Jason Shmyr's single-season record for fighting majors.

Unlike Shmyr, who was a pure fighting machine, born and bred to seek out and destroy all who stood in his way, Doull took more of a philosophical approach to his role.

"Whatever pays the bills and whatever helps my team win, that's what I'll do,"[9] said Doull.

To Doull, fighting was just an easy way to make a living.

"What's a fight last? Forty seconds to a minute? That's a minute out of your day … and you get paid pretty good money to do it."

"I'm still making a name, too, where I'm trying to look for well-known fighters."[9]

He would indeed find plenty of well-known fighters to establish his reputation. With Doull leading the way, no team in the league would fight more than the Moose this year. Unfortunately, unlike what happened in *Slap Shot*, all that fighting wouldn't help the Moose win.

"Frustration is high right now,"[10] said Brian Chapman as the Moose's woes continued through December. Their fortunes took another hit when Bohonos slid into the boards and broke his ankle, forcing the league's leading scorer to the sidelines for more than six weeks. Only their goaltending would keep the Moose from going into a complete free fall. Manny Legace struggled in his first few games after his late arrival, but he soon settled down, and alongside Jason Elliott, they consistently provided the Moose with solid, steady netminding.

In their first game after Christmas, Wayne Armstrong of nearby Headingley, an adult, was chosen as the Moose's millionth fan and awarded a trip for two to a road game next year. It would have been far more fitting for that fan to have been an eight-year-old boy, or even more appropriately, an empty seat.

As part of my mini-pack, the Moose had given me a voucher for a free ticket to use during an early-January home stand. I gave the voucher to my mother, who attended what would be her first and only Moose game.

In a game where she got in on a free ticket, she saw a fight and a low-scoring contest in which the offensively challenged Moose lost in a shootout. It was truly the Manitoba Moose in a microcosm.

Trying to shake up the team, the Moose traded feisty Jason MacDonald to Orlando for 28-year-old defenseman Terry Hollinger, but the beat went on for the floundering Moose. Just when they appeared to be on the threshold of breaking out of their malaise, a few bad games would knock them back down to square one. Even within games, they'd play well for a period, then seemingly take the next period off.

"But right now we'll play well for 10 and then take 10 off. That's been our problem. We can't put a solid 60 minutes together,"[11] said Prokopec.

In late January, the Moose visited the Cleveland Lumberjacks in what was to be a special night to honor Jock Callander, who had recently eclipsed Len Thornson's all-time IHL point record.

Or so it seemed.

After some meticulous digging through archives of *The Hockey News* and the *Muskegon Chronicle*, Tim Campbell of the *Free Press* discovered a typo that resulted in Callander incorrectly being credited with an additional 13 points. The IHL admitted that Campbell was indeed correct and that Callander had not actually set the record, forcing postponement of the festivities.

It was embarrassing for Callander, the Lumberjacks and the league, but Callander would shortly break Thornson's record again, this time for good, and receive his well-earned honors.

In fairness, these types of statistical errors were not unique to the IHL. During my research for my first two books on the Jets, I found numerous errors in both the official statistics and in their media guides. I suspect Callander's case might just be the tip of an iceberg that few in the game are aware of.

Months later, Campbell would devote some ink in his column to railing on the stats posted on the IHL's Web site. Campbell might have been better served to turn his attention in-house, since his own employer was no less guilty of the same issues he fingered others for.

In publishing game summaries, the *Free Press* often omitted the list of shooters in a shootout, the game officials and the player who served a bench or goaltender penalty. Even important details about an injury to a Moose player or a new acquisition would not appear in the *Free Press* for several days, if at all.

At the end of January, Campbell penned a short article on me and my Moose site based on an interview he did with me earlier in the month. Under the headline of "Moose fan calls it like he sees it on his Web site," Campbell detailed all the features on my site and, in particular, drew attention to my "View from Section 26" opinion column.

Given my publicly stated contempt for his employer, I was shocked when Campbell first contacted me. On my Jets site, I laid part of the blame for the Jets' departure on the *Free Press* for badmouthing the Spirit of Manitoba group, who were putting together a last-ditch effort in the spring of 1995 to purchase the club and keep it in Winnipeg.

In addition, I had always resented the *Free Press* for trying to influence public opinion rather than reporting on it. The *Free Press* was and remains the province's biggest private-sector purveyor of left-wing political propaganda. To this day, I scoff at those who call the *Free Press* a "newspaper."

Nonetheless, I still agreed to talk to Campbell. He was one of their few reporters who took a more objective view, and he generally avoided the quick rush to judgment that his colleagues were more known for.

I would appear in the *Free Press* four more times over the coming years, but none of those occasions would involve the Moose.

In early February, the Moose hosted Long Beach for a pair of games over the weekend. In Saturday's opener, more than 3,000 additional children were airlifted in from northern Manitoba to supplement the normally high concentration of the Moose's favored demographic. Paid for by various government agencies and Crown corporations, "Aboriginal Youth Night" would sadly become an annual event.

The Moose were lethargic that night, but the same could not be said for the children who were seated next to me. I spent the night being kicked, prodded and jabbed by a group of particularly rambunctious children who screamed and hollered throughout the contest. With every seat taken, there was nowhere else left for me to escape but home.

On the surface, bringing in these kids may have seemed like a noble gesture, but by accepting this taxpayer-funded sellout crowd, the Moose again likely had done more to turn away current and future ticket buyers. No doubt, if Chipman had to sit alongside these children instead of watching from a distance in the press box or in a private suite, this is an event that would not have been repeated.

Backstopped by former Jets goaltender Nikolai Khabibulin, the Ice Dogs completed the sweep the next day. Sitting in the middle of a much tamer crowd, seeing Khabibulin was the highlight of an otherwise forgettable weekend.

It would be more of the same for the Moose, who continued to lose, but rarely did they go down without a fight. In the finale of a two-game set in Orlando, master agitator Jimmy Roy touched off another brawl in which both goaltenders eventually became involved. Two players, including Roy, were ejected.

Scoring for the Solar Bears in the opener was Atlanta Thrashers prospect Dan Snyder, who was in his first pro season. Snyder would work his way up to the NHL only to be tragically killed in a car crash days before the start of the 2003-2004 season. A passenger in a car driven by teammate Dany Heatley, he was ejected from the speeding vehicle and died six days later, never regaining consciousness.

Beginning that season, the Thrashers presented the Dan Snyder Memorial Award to the player who "best embodies perseverance, dedication, and hard work without reward or recognition, so that his team and teammates might succeed." Chipman would continue the award after purchasing the Thrashers and moving them to Winnipeg in 2011.

As the team staggered to the finish line, the Moose sent out a letter to their season ticket and mini-pack holders.

"In seven short weeks our team will begin the quest to bring a Turner Cup and a professional sports championship to Manitoba in this, our fourth season in the league."[12]

Not surprisingly, this "quest" would again be short-lived.

In addition to detailing the IHL's laughably inclusive playoff format, the Moose also offered the opportunity for season ticket and mini-pack holders to guarantee their seats for the postseason. Expecting to have to pre-pay for the package, I was shocked to read they would process payments after the playoffs. I called Kristy the next day and gave her the verbal equivalent of an IOU.

A Friday night date with Chicago at the Arena drew the Moose's first legitimate sellout in over two years, but despite the unusually large turnout, they still went down 2-0 in yet another subpar effort.

Still searching for the right mix, the Moose made a couple of more deals. They picked up NHL veterans Shawn Burr and Dan Kesa on loan from the Tampa Bay Lightning, then they traded Patrice Tardif to the AHL's Quebec Citadelles for defenseman Barry Richter.

Richter was a big, mobile defenseman who had played 23 NHL games this year, but the much bigger benefit of the trade for the Moose was getting rid of Tardif. He was not having a terribly productive season, and combined with his odd personality, his departure was truly a case of addition by subtraction.

Off the ice, however, I would find myself missing Tardif. His eccentric behavior made even the most dull game interesting, and in many respects, Moose hockey was just not the same without characters like him.

All three newcomers made their Moose debut in the first of a two-game weekend series against the Blades, but Kesa suffered a devastating knee injury in the first period and would be lost for the season.

Late in the opener of a three-game road trip, Eric Veilleux narrowly avoided a similar fate after he was knocked down by former Moose Neil Brady's high stick. While he was still lying on the ice, it was only Burr's last-second yell that enabled him to duck out of the way as an enraged Brady attempted to cross-check him in the head. Sadly, this would be Burr's only significant contribution to the Moose.

In mid-March, I was one of about a few hundred who attended the Moose's fan forum. In addition to snapping a few pictures during a dressing room tour, I watched and listened from a distance as Chipman and Carlyle answered questions from the fans.

The most noteworthy moment of the night came from one fan who asked Chipman a very pointed question about the level of press coverage the Moose had been receiving. Even in this, their fourth season in Winnipeg, the Moose had hardly been given any attention on radio, television, or either of the *Free Press* or the *Winnipeg Sun*. Chipman was clearly and justifiably displeased with the lack of coverage, but he adeptly danced around the question with the dexterity of a career politician.

At the IHL's trading deadline, the Moose shipped the recently acquired Terry Hollinger to the AHL's Providence Bruins for 29-year-old centerman Sean Pronger and 26-year-old defenseman Keith McCambridge.

A minor-league journeyman, Pronger was best known as the older brother of NHL All-Star defenseman Chris Pronger. He would, however, soon carve out a reputation all his own while with the Moose. He quickly established himself as one of the team leaders, and his work ethic was beyond reproach. Unfortunately, he was so bereft of hockey skills that he made Mike Prokopec look like a veritable Baryshnikov on skates.

He was excruciatingly slow, and no player in Moose history would gas more golden scoring opportunities than Pronger. Yet Carlyle would send Pronger over the boards time and again when the Moose were on a power play. Pronger's presence on the ice would be akin to waiving the man advantage.

It was only his leadership, work ethic and last name that had kept him in pro hockey for so long.

McCambridge would do little but provide some depth on the blue line. Interestingly, however, he would go on to coach the franchise after Chipman had moved it to St. John's following his purchase of the Thrashers.

As the Moose's hold on a playoff position became increasingly tenuous, their fortunes took another turn for the worse when they lost Prokopec to a season-ending injury in the same game in Long Beach.

Three nights later, in a 4-2 loss to the Blades in Kansas City, Burr called Dody Wood a "dumb Indian"[15] during a fracas at the Moose bench. Burr would later be fined by the league for the incident and ordered to personally apologize to Wood, who was of Aboriginal heritage. The image-conscious Chipman, meanwhile, publicly apologized to all Manitoba Aboriginals as well as Rod Bushie, Grand Chief of the Assembly of Manitoba Chiefs.

Back home, the Moose picked up a pair of wins over the league's second-worst team to salt away the fifth and final playoff position in the Western Conference. The Moose closed out the regular season with a pair of weekend games against Long Beach, their opponents in the first round of the upcoming playoffs.

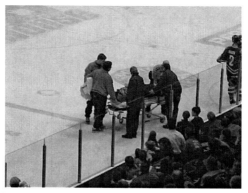

Rusty Fitzgerald being taken off on a stretcher.[1]

In Friday's opener, the Ice Dogs went head hunting and sent both Jim Montgomery and Rusty Fitzgerald off the ice on stretchers, sparking a record-setting emotional battle. The seven fights that followed not only set a single-game Moose record but also enabled the Moose to pass the century mark in fighting majors for the first time in team history.

The Moose won by a score of 6-1, but though Fitzgerald would return in the playoffs, Montgomery was done for the year.

All that emotion fizzled out quickly the following night as the Moose dropped a lackluster 5-1 decision before an overflow crowd.

"I don't feel very good about my hockey team tonight,"[13] said Carlyle.

Nor would he for the rest of the year.

The best-of-three preliminary-round series began at the Arena, where the Ice Dogs easily won by a score of 5-2 in front of a much more customary paltry and disinterested gathering. Two nights later in Long Beach, the Moose put up a bit of a struggle, but they went down 3-2 on a goal in the second overtime period to put an end to what had been a miserably disappointing season. Expecting to seriously challenge for the Turner Cup, the Moose again reverted to being one of the league's bottom-feeders and were promptly swept out of the playoffs.

"I don't think we really came together as a team,"[14] said Carlyle in summing up the year.

Only a microscopic upswing in fan interest kept the season from being a complete write-off. Even that slight increase, however, would prove to be a blip in a downward spiral that would resume its regular course next year.

It was back to the old drawing board.

2000-2001: The End of an Era

With absolutely nothing to show for their first four years in Manitoba, the Moose listlessly prepared to embark on their fifth. On the ice, they had been little more than also-rans, and off the ice, they had been willing victims of a tidal wave of apathy and indifference. In many respects, it was surprising the team was still in business.

A week after the season, I received a letter in the mail from the Moose detailing their Team Builder Program. "Established in 1998 as a small group of committed supporters working to help increase our season ticket subscriptions,"[1] this program was designed to have customers drum up business for the Moose. For each referral, fans would earn points they could redeem for Moose merchandise.

"If each Manitoba Moose season ticket holder drafts one friend, you will be helping to fill the arena!"

"Bigger crowds, greater excitement, and you helped!"

"All it takes is one! So draft a friend … we'll do the rest!"[1]

In other words, we can't fill the building. Maybe our customers can.

It is the epitome of desperation when a pro sports team appeals to its fans to become salesmen, not to mention a shameful abdication of responsibility to market the team. Combined with the ever-declining attendance and the pending expiration of their Arena lease, it looked increasingly likely that this would be the Moose's last season in Winnipeg.

On the front cover of the color brochure promoting the Team Builder Program, the Moose unveiled their marketing slogan, "For the Love of the Game." Love of the game wasn't the problem in Winnipeg. Love of this team was.

In addition to asking their fans to become salesmen, the Moose would later ask fans to become ushers as well. The so-called Fan Patrol program would see the Moose replace one of the two disinterested paid ushers at each ramp with an equally lackadaisical volunteer.

It was astounding that the Moose were able to find enough free labor to stock each ramp. It was becoming increasingly hard enough to get people to come and watch the games for free, let alone asking them to work while they were there. It would be a sad statement that this bit of miserly scrimping would stand as one of the organization's most clever moves of all time.

As Rome burned, so to speak, Mark Chipman instead devoted his energies to wooing the Vancouver Canucks. Chipman badly wanted the Moose to serve as the Canucks' affiliate, but negotiations broke down over Chipman's desire to retain Randy Carlyle as the coach. Vancouver had instead insisted that Stan Smyl, a former Canucks player and a longtime member of the organization, lead their prospects.

Canucks general manager Brian Burke would later state, "It was definitely a stumbling block in the discussions we have had prior to this season."[16]

"Popular belief that has never been shot down is that any previous consideration of an affiliation deal for the Moose always included Carlyle as a main player in the arrangement,"[2] wrote Tim Campbell in the *Free Press*.

Speaking on a CJOB radio interview during the season, Chipman would admit his reeling team could have saved $750,000 on an affiliation deal with the Canucks, an amount which was more than half of the Moose's entire payroll. Instead, he turned his back on what would have been a financial windfall to retain a coach who had delivered two bottom-half finishes in three full seasons on the job along with three straight quick exits from the playoffs. Blind loyalty to "Captain Crony" clearly took precedence over all other priorities.

The Canucks, meanwhile, moved on and inked a one-year affiliation agreement with the rival Blades.

The Moose then began remaking their roster with an eye towards addressing what had gone so badly wrong the year before.

"We made some mistakes in putting together our team last year when we focused on skill over work ethic or character or whatever description you want,"[4] said Carlyle.

Their first moves were to pick up three players from the defunct Ice Dogs, one of two more teams to leave the IHL during the summer. The Cincinnati Cyclones looked like they would make it three, but they ultimately decided to continue operating.

Returning players included captain Brian Chapman, reigning Moose MVP Brett Hauer, Rusty Fitzgerald, Dan Kesa, Justin Kurtz, Jeff Parrott, Sean Pronger, Jimmy Roy, Mike Ruark and, of course, Cory Cyrenne.

Parrott, however, would not see the ice this year for the Moose. Hinting at some issues with the prickly Carlyle, Parrott said, "I'm not his type of player."[3] After spending the first month of the season in the press box, Parrott stated the obvious when he said, "I don't know how to say this nicely, but my days are done here … even if there were five injuries."[3]

Days later, he would be mercifully assigned to the Border City Bandits of the Central Hockey League.

It was an odd and classless send-off for a well-respected and long-tenured player who had been an unheralded but important member of the team on and off the ice. Two years earlier, Parrott had been named the team's unsung hero and last year, he was the corecipient of the team's community service award.

Unfortunately, his case would not be the last of a Moose player who had given so much to the team only to be dumped in an unceremonious fashion.

Leaving the Moose were Michael Stewart, Lonny Bohonos, Jim Montgomery, Bill Bowler, Mike Prokopec and fighter Doug Doull. To replace Doull, the Moose signed Mel Angelstad, unquestionably the most renowned fighter in minor-league hockey. The 2,775 penalty minutes he had racked up over the course of 469 pro games could hardly begin to tell his story.

When in Winnipeg as a visiting player, "Mad Mel" would proudly boast about his fighting numbers like a sniper would list his goal-scoring exploits. His annual totals in the 30s and 40s dwarfed Doull's franchise-high mark of 20 last year and Jason Shmyr's previous record of 18, set two years earlier.

More than the numbers, however, Angelstad was an entertainer and the ultimate folk hero. No one in the game at this level could match his magnetism and star power. He was born in Saskatchewan, but he was made purely for Hollywood. No Academy Award–winning screen writer could possibly have written a better character than Mel Angelstad.

After his first fight with the Moose, in a bit of showmanship that would come to define his career, he tipped his helmet and beamed his childlike grin at a woman who was pounding on the glass nearby.

Though Angelstad treated the rink like his personal movie set, he was a champion prize fighter who was feared around the league. Of his hundreds of fights, rarely did an opponent get the best of him. In addition, unlike past fighters the Moose have had, he had some semblance of hockey skills. During this coming season, he would be pressed into duty on the blue line on occasion and acquit himself well.

The Moose made a number of other additions including former Jets defenseman Bobby Dollas and former Moose players Scott Thomas and Johan Hedberg, as well as 27-year-old defenseman Philippe Boucher. Unfortunately, Dollas and Thomas would attract NHL interest and neither would spend much time with the Moose this year but Hedberg and Boucher would each make a more significant contribution.

On loan from the San Jose Sharks, Hedberg was inconsistent in his first go-round with the Moose, but he would be much, much better this time around.

A former NHL first-round draft choice, Boucher had once been a regular with the Los Angeles Kings, but he had missed much of last season due to a series of injuries. Fully healthy, he would shine during the first half of the year before his recall to Los Angeles.

With every former NHL player that had been assigned to the Moose, it would generally not take me very long to figure out why he was in the minors and not in the NHL. Watching Boucher night after night, I never found that reason. He was an NHL-quality player and would be one of the most impressive players to ever don a Moose uniform. Not surprisingly, he would go on to enjoy a long career in the NHL, most notably with the Dallas Stars.

Spurned in their efforts to hook up with the Canucks, the Moose would again turn to the Detroit Red Wings, who would provide them with a few players as part of their unofficial partial affiliation. Among them were a pair of centermen, Steve Brule and Bruce Richardson. Brule had been one of the top scorers for the AHL's Albany River Rats over the past five seasons, while the gritty Richardson had bounced around across the minor leagues over the last three years.

The Moose were also supposed to get goaltender Manny Legace, but he unexpectedly beat out 14-year NHL veteran Ken Wregget for the job as Chris Osgood's backup. As a result, the Red Wings would instead send Wregget to the Moose.

The last-minute switch seemed inconsequential for the Moose at the time. Wregget had a resume with impeccable credentials, and though he was on the downside of his career, the Moose were still likely getting a quality IHL-caliber goaltender.

Or so I thought.

With Wregget in the final year of a lucrative one-way deal, the Red Wings would be forced to pay him his full salary of $850,000 not to play for them. It would prove to be money well spent for the Red Wings, but costly to the Moose in terms of wins and losses.

Around the league, aside from the Blades, three more of the IHL's remaining 11 teams became full NHL affiliates, reversing a trend that had seen the IHL become almost completely independent. In a case of "monkey see, monkey do," the IHL also decided to copy the NHL and adopt the four-on-four overtime format to decide tied games in advance of a shootout.

I would find it odd that many of the hockey purists who so virulently opposed the shootout, including Chipman, wholeheartedly endorsed this new proposal. Proponents argued that by taking one skater off the ice in a format in which there was nothing to lose, since each team was guaranteed a point in the standings, that a much more wide-open style of play would result. Indeed it would, but it was no more a natural part of the game than the shootout, and it would be just as much of a slapstick made-for-television gimmick.

Sadly, this new overtime format would become a fixture at all levels of hockey in the years to come.

The Moose would return to local television after inking an eight-game television package with A-Channel. This was the same station that, years earlier, had indirectly mocked the Moose in promoting their coverage of Edmonton Oilers games.

While the Moose were going through training camp, the Arena played host to its first taste of NHL action in five years when the Minnesota Wild met the Canucks in an exhibition game. I was among the crowd of 11,539 in attendance to see the Wild go down 4-0 to the Canucks that afternoon.

In front of me in line at the front doors was a gentleman who remarked, "I haven't been here since the Jets left."

Based on the reaction from the crowd, he was not alone. Former Jets goaltender Bob Essensa earned the shutout for Vancouver, and chants of "Bob-ee" sprang up when Essensa would make a save. This recognition of Essensa's presence was in sharp contrast to the many former Jets who had been virtually ignored when they had come in to face the Moose. It was yet another strong indicator as to how unsuccessful the Moose had been in their feeble efforts to attract former Jets fans.

At center ice that afternoon was the Moose's fifth anniversary logo complete with the slogan "MADE IN CANADA" underneath. After seeing it, I wondered if I had missed the announcement that Minnesota had switched its national allegiance from the U.S. to Canada, since the Moose had played their first two seasons there.

The more likely possibility, however, was that the Moose organization either conveniently overlooked or forgot that little detail about where the team had been founded.

In their final tune-up before the regular season, the Moose dropped a 5-1 fight-filled affair to the defending Turner Cup champion Wolves. After the game, Carlyle had this to say on all the fighting throughout the exhibition season:

"I don't think that's the trademark of this hockey club. I don't think we as an organization want that to be. We want to play a good, tough aggressive brand of hockey and the other stuff is best left on the street or the back alley."[5]

Those were hollow words from the coach of a team that had just signed the biggest celebrity fighter in the game and led the league in fighting majors last season.

After a pair of losses on the road to begin the regular season, the Moose dropped their third straight before a sparse gathering of just over 5,000 in their home opener. The Moose quickly righted the ship, however, and backstopped by Hedberg's stellar goaltending, they won six in a row before meeting Orlando for a pair of weekend games in mid-November.

The Moose took both games, but the two victories were easily overshadowed by a heavyweight bout on Saturday night between Angelstad and up-and-coming challenger Darcy Hordichuk. The two staged an epic slugfest in the league opener, and the rematch was no less of a classic.

Angelstad took the bout in a split decision, but Hordichuk proved himself a worthy adversary as both fighters furiously traded haymakers. After the game, Hordichuk expressed his gratitude to Angelstad:

"For a guy trying to get a reputation in this league, I really appreciate that a veteran like that would fight me."[6]

Darcy Hordichuk vs. Mel Angelstad.[1]

For good measure, Angelstad also scored the game-winner in the contest, netting what would be his only goal as a member of the Moose.

Early the following week, the Moose picked up 14-year NHL veteran John MacLean to bolster their lineup. After more than a decade with the New Jersey Devils, MacLean had signed a lucrative free-agent contract with the Rangers two years ago, one of many big contracts the Rangers would seek to rid themselves of. Hoping he would retire and save them from paying his $2.5 million salary, the Rangers banished him to Winnipeg, but MacLean would not oblige and surprised many by reporting to the Moose. He would do anything but sulk, and armed with an upbeat attitude, "Johnny Mac" would be a great fit for the Moose.

The Moose's winning streak ended at 10 with a loss in Chicago, but as always, they didn't go down without a fight. In the third period, Paul Kruse of the Wolves instigated a scrap with Angelstad, marking the first of two consecutive days in which a player resorted to taking a penalty to pick a fight with the Moose's famed pugilist. Angelstad was perhaps the most willing combatant in the game and hardly needed prodding. It was probably the only time in Angelstad's career where someone had taken a penalty to get him to drop the gloves.

Angelstad's opponent the following evening was Chris Neil as the Moose entertained the Grand Rapids Griffins at the Arena. Unlike Hordichuk, Neil wasn't just another eager greenhorn looking for a reputation. In addition to his toughness, he could also handle himself with the gloves on, which had become a necessary skill set for prospective fighters at the NHL level. Neil would indeed earn a call-up the following season and would go on to enjoy a lengthy career with the Ottawa Senators.

Before the NHL would come calling, however, Neil had to contend with Angelstad and the Moose in a rematch at the Arena two weeks later. In a rare appearance, the Moose's marketing department took notice and placed a big ad in the *Free Press* in the days leading up to the game promoting this prospective "Heavyweight Battle." In the ad designed like a fight card, they paired off the two would-be combatants, listing their height, weight and penalty minute totals. In addition, the Moose had 2,000 posters printed featuring Angelstad, adorned with a deep cut on his face suffered in the fight with Kruse, sitting on top of a motorcycle with the caption, "You can run, but you can't hide."

There was instant fallout from the ad and the Moose were forced to hastily backtrack. Even the IHL, a league with little moral standing to criticize the overt promotion of fighting, took a dim view of what the Moose had done.

"We're not marketing fighting on our hockey team,"[7] claimed Tim Scott, the Moose's vice president of sales and marketing.

"We realized right away it wasn't an accurate reflection of what we're all about. So we said, 'Let's change it,'"[7] said Chipman.

Unfortunately, it *was* an accurate reflection of what the Moose were all about. Fighting was regularly overshadowing the Moose's mediocre play, and furthermore, it was exactly what their preferred demographic, elementary school children, wanted to see.

Nonetheless, in response to the public outcry, they did change the ad the next day. They replaced the fight card portion of the ad with a comparison of the two teams' records, power plays and penalty-killing units, but they still went ahead with the poster giveaway.

In spite of all the publicity, most of it bad, an announced crowd of fewer than 6,000 showed up and I didn't exactly have to ward off a throng of overeager Angelstad admirers to claim my poster. It remains one of my most prized pieces of memorabilia from that era.

Ironically, the game itself, won by the Moose 3-1, was one of the tamest in Moose history. Not only did Angelstad and Neil not drop the gloves, but there were few signs of any ill will between the two teams all night long. In fact, the 10 penalty minutes assessed in the contest would be the fifth-lowest total of any Moose game during their years in the IHL.

The Moose took three of five on the home stand and remained in top spot in the Western Conference, yet attendance and interest in the team were bottoming out. Crowd figures were often announced in the 6,000-7,000 range but on most nights, there were fewer than 4,000 actually in the building. Even Randy Carlyle took the unusual step of publicly bemoaning the lack of fan support.

Despite the thinning crowds, I began to notice two new regulars nearby. Three rows behind me in the aisle seats was a mother in her mid-40s along with her teenage daughter. They were undoubtedly two of the most keenly interested fans in the building, and the daughter might also have been the only child in the Arena who was accompanied by a parent.

They were well behaved and kept to themselves, but the mother would spend most of the game giving a running play-by-play and shouting encouragement to the players. It almost sounded like she was trying out to become Kelly Moore's replacement. She wasn't exceptionally loud, but with the building so empty, I could easily hear every word she was saying. It wouldn't have surprised me if the players could hear her as well.

After splitting a four-game road trip, the Moose returned home to begin a five-game home stand that would take them into the new year. Before taking on the Aeros on December 22, the Moose held a 40-minute pregame ceremony honoring Dale Hawerchuk, the greatest player the Jets had during their 17 seasons in the NHL.

Dale Hawerchuk Night.[1]

The Moose had announced this event two weeks earlier, prompting a stampede to the box office, and the game quickly sold out.

No doubt, they had some honorable motives in paying tribute to one of the greatest players in Jets history. Chipman had been part of the Save the Jets efforts, and the loss of the team probably hurt him as much as it did any other devoted Winnipeg hockey fan. Honoring Hawerchuk may have been seen as a chance to say goodbye to a beloved legend and help heal an old wound that had been festering in the hearts of so many Winnipeggers. However, with the Moose struggling so badly at the gate, it would be difficult to suggest this was something other than a cheap promotional ploy.

In addition, Chipman spoiled what should have been a joyous celebration by inviting Winnipeg mayor Glen Murray to stand alongside Hawerchuk at center ice.

Glen Murray was a man with a grand vision for the city and was doggedly determined to implement his ideas regardless of cost or public opinion. Unabashedly arrogant and rude, he quickly established himself as one of the most controversial and polarizing political figures in the province's history.

During the fight to save the Jets five years earlier, Murray had actively supported Thin Ice, a social activist group that was opposed to the use of public funding for a new arena that would have kept the Jets in Winnipeg. In effect, Murray was there celebrating the history of a team he helped send packing.

Chipman could not have chosen a more inappropriate person to be part of the ceremony, and inviting Murray was perhaps his most shameful act during his ownership of the Moose. Rather than healing an old wound, Murray's presence served only to rip it wide open and rub salt in it.

The Turner Cup, symbol of IHL supremacy, was on a league-wide tour, and I got to see it for the first time during this home stand.

I had expected to find it behind a glass case, guarded by a security detail wearing white gloves, much like how the Stanley Cup was handled. Instead, it was left sitting at the end of a banquet table identified only by a piece of paper with the words "Turner Cup" handwritten on it, stuck to the trophy with a piece of Scotch tape. With only one of Chipman's disinterested staffers nearby nominally standing guard, it was a minor miracle it wasn't stolen.

Turner Cup.[10]

Had it been snatched, it would not have been the first time the Cup had disappeared. Ever since being purchased at the Lawrence Trophy Center in Detroit for $500 a half-century earlier, it has seemingly taken on a life of its own. Perhaps the most bizarre story involving the Cup came when an inebriated Jim Playfair slipped with it in his hand during a championship celebration in 1990. The Cup broke in three places and was put back together with Elmer's Glue.

Following the largely successful home stand, Tim Campbell penned an editorial in which he stated, "The doomsayers and statistically challenged have obviously had a busy holiday season, certainly too busy to notice or comment on a sharp turnaround in attendance at the Arena for Manitoba Moose games."[8]

Since the number of people who cared enough to publicly comment on the team besides the paid scribes numbered somewhere between zero and one, I took the liberty of assuming that Campbell's volley was aimed squarely at me.

Campbell was indeed correct when he noted there had been an upswing in attendance during the home stand. However, in his apparent zeal to take a shot at me, he cast aside one of the cardinal rules of journalism – to be a doubting Thomas and take a hard look at the real reason behind this "sharp turnaround."

A major factor in the rosier attendance figures was Dale Hawerchuk Night, which attracted a sellout crowd. All the seats had legitimately been sold, but the crowd was on hand to see Hawerchuk, not the Moose. Hawerchuk's appearance would likely have drawn a sellout if there had not even been a game that night. One night earlier, the announced crowd was 5,356, but in reality, there were only around 3,500 fans in attendance, perhaps the lowest total in Moose history.

Furthermore, with the exception of the taxpayer-funded Aboriginal Youth Night that would follow in February, this would be the Moose's only sellout crowd during the regular season.

There were larger than normal crowds at the next two games of the home stand, but the New Year's Eve contest, which traditionally draws a near sellout, attracted a crowd of only 8,453. That figure ranked second-lowest among the Moose's four New Year's Eve dates.

Even taking these attendance figures at face value, it only brought the average up to last year's level, which was hardly anything to crow about, nor did it reflect an upward trend of interest in the team. Thus, there was no reason for me to comment on it.

As I expected, this "sharp turnaround" would come to an abrupt halt. The next home game drew an announced crowd of only 5,360, with around 1,500 of those coming disguised as empty seats, details that Campbell failed to mention. Perhaps he was too busy.

Tim Campbell is an astute reporter, one who normally stands above his colleagues. This was one rare occasion in which he did not.

The Moose cooled off following their strong start to the season, but they still maintained a solid grip on first place as they prepared to host the Admirals in a Saturday night tilt at the Arena. The Moose utterly dominated the contest, but Admirals goaltender Jan Lasak stood on his head and single-handedly stole the game for his team.

On cue, with one minute to play, a regular seated a dozen rows in front of me pulled out a cigarette from his pack of Old Port and lit up. An elderly man likely in his 70s, he was a stout figure no taller than 5-foot-2 with an enormous pot belly, a puffy face and a bald head. My good friend Steve would later take one glance at him and adorn him with the moniker "Bubba."

Smoking had long since been prohibited in the seating area and even in most parts of the concourse, yet over the last few games, Bubba brazenly began lighting up in his seat near the end of the game. Seated by his lonesome at eye level between two separate pairs of ushers, he couldn't have been any easier to spot, yet none of these ushers would say a word to him.

I made no fewer than three separate calls to Kristy Nykoluk, my account representative, and though I received a sympathetic ear and repeated assurances that it would be taken care of, nothing was done. On this particular night, six ushers were standing around watching him puff away.

Getting nowhere through my primary contact with the Moose, I went over her head and fired off an e-mail to Mark Chipman the following morning. Only then was this matter finally addressed. At the next home game, one of the nearby ushers made the bold move to approach him, and I would never again spot him smoking in the stands.

In all probability, Bubba knew how indolent Chipman's staffers were just as well as I did. He could have done just about anything without their batting an eye. It was only his misfortune in sharing the same section as someone with an allergy who also had a direct pipeline to the owner that stopped him from making this a much more regular practice.

I would later spot Bubba shining shoes in an underground mall in downtown Winnipeg. He remained at that same location for years until both he and his shoe shine stand disappeared. I never did find out what happened to him, but he was anything but a picture of health and, obviously having been such a heavy smoker, I suspect he is no longer with us.

The wheels slowly began to come off for the Moose as they lost five in a row. The smoke and mirrors act that was the backbone of their offensive attack at last began faltering, and only Johan Hedberg's goaltending was holding them above water.

"It's just a lot of little parts gone awry,"[9] said Carlyle on the slump.

More bad news came when the Rangers traded John MacLean to the Dallas Stars. MacLean got the news he would be returning to the NHL while ice fishing with his teammates on an off-day in nearby Lockport.

Meanwhile, the losing continued and their hold on first place grew more tenuous with each passing day. Carlyle tried shaking up the lineup, but nothing seemed to work.

The day after another disheartening, sparsely attended defeat on home ice, the Moose held their second annual Season Ticket Holder Appreciation Night. I was one of a crowd generously estimated by the *Free Press* at 2,500, not much less than the number in attendance at the game the previous night.

The highlight of the dressing room tour was seeing the children swarm around Angelstad like he was Santa Claus. He was the only player who attracted any significant attention from the children, and Carlyle was the only other person in the room to draw a gathering.

Mel Angelstad signs autographs.[1]

The crowd in attendance.[1]

Kelly Moore at the podium. Seated are Jimmy Roy, Mark Chipman and Randy Carlyle.[1]

I didn't even have to ward off anyone when approaching Chipman following the question and answer session. He was polite during what was our first and only meeting.

The Moose hit the road and wound up a miserable four-game swing with a 9-2 blowout defeat in Cincinnati that knocked them back into a share of first place. After landing at the Winnipeg airport, Carlyle got a call informing him that the Sharks had recalled Hedberg and traded him to the Pittsburgh Penguins. In a scene eerily reminiscent of the Richard Shulmistra affair two years earlier, the Moose instantly lost their best player at the worst possible time.

"This is never good to happen but we're fortunate enough to have the resource of a 17-year veteran goaltender in Ken Wregget,"[10] said Carlyle, trying desperately to put a positive spin on the devastating news.

"Fortunate" was not a sentiment I felt in describing Wregget's presence on the Moose roster. He had been having a miserable year and seemingly never recovered from an early-season injury. In the rout in Cincinnati, he had been torched for six of the nine goals and again looked awful in the Moose net. Though he had not yet seen much action this year, his play would not improve with more playing time in the last month of the regular season.

Hedberg's loss would indeed prove catastrophic for the Moose, but his arrival in Pittsburgh would kick off a lengthy and successful NHL career for the popular and classy Swede. He would quickly earn the starter's role and become a cult hero as he led the Penguins deep into the playoffs. Still wearing his mask from the Moose, Pittsburgh fans took to yelling "Moose" after a brilliant save, and the moniker would follow him for the remainder of his career.

To back up Wregget for the rest of the year, the Moose again called on minor-league journeyman Jeff Salajko from the ECHL. The quintessential "rent-a-goalie," he had filled in for the Moose as well as other IHL teams in past years. A fifth-year pro, Salajko had more stickers on his suitcase than most travel agents and the Moose would not be the first team he had been with for a second time. Have stick, will travel. Often.

After the Moose dropped their first two games following Hedberg's recall, Salajko made his first start, replacing an ineffective Wregget. Salajko was outstanding in a 38-save performance, but the Moose still lost 2-1 as his offensively challenged teammates gave him no support.

The following night, Wregget returned to the net and played surprisingly well as the Moose rebounded for a 3-2 win over Utah. The headline attraction of the night for those few fans in attendance, however, was a first-period scrap between Angelstad and former Moose fighter Jason Shmyr. It marked the first fight between a current and former Moose heavyweight champion, and fittingly, it ended in a draw.

Mel Angelstad vs. Jason Shmyr.[1]

The Moose somehow maintained their hold on first place, but the rest of the West was catching up quickly. In late March, only six points separated first from the fourth and final playoff position.

"We're very concerned. We have reason to be concerned,"[11] said Carlyle, who himself would soon become the primary reason for that concern.

Salajko backstopped the Moose to a weekend sweep of the Aeros and earned Goaltender of the Week honors in the IHL, but Carlyle would soon turn back to Wregget.

"We'll try and see which direction we're going to go. Success will obviously dictate that,"[12] said Carlyle on his fragile goaltending situation. Unfortunately, blind loyalty would take precedence over success.

The losses kept piling up, and in early April, even a playoff berth that once seemed a virtual certainty was now in jeopardy. Wregget continued to struggle, yet Carlyle kept playing him. In a Sunday afternoon loss to a Kansas City team playing out the string, Wregget yielded four goals on 15 shots before being mercifully replaced in favor of Salajko.

It was sad to see this proud veteran at the end of a long and distinguished career playing so poorly and embarrassing himself. No doubt, each bad goal hurt him even more than it did me or any other fan. He was giving it his all, but he just had nothing left to give.

Wregget's struggles mirrored those of former Jet Joe Daley, who was at the end of his outstanding career late in the 1978-1979 season.

"He looked like a goaltender who has played the game too long but not enough lately ... if that makes any sense,"[13] was the way *Free Press* reporter Reyn Davis summed up Daley's play at the time. He could have used those same words in talking about Wregget more than two decades later.

Nonetheless, Carlyle continued to put his team's playoff chances in mortal peril by starting Wregget so often. Salajko was not a top-flight IHL goaltender, but he was at least healthy, and more often than not, he gave his team a chance to win.

Late in the season, a rare visitor to my site signed my guestbook. A big fan of Wregget, she posted an entry in which she used the line "Can I say how much I love this site?" I suspect she posted the entry long before reading some of my commentary in which I let my anger get the better of me in expressing my frustration over Carlyle's obstinance in starting Wregget night after night.

The point they received in a shootout loss in Cincinnati enabled the Moose to back into a playoff berth. A win in the regular-season finale would still have allowed the Moose to claim home ice advantage in the first round of the playoffs, but they responded with one of their worst performances of the season and went down 3-0. It was the ninth time this season the Moose had been shut out, and as a result of the loss, they were forced to open their first-round best-of-seven series with the Aeros in Houston.

Salajko started the series opener, but after three early goals, Carlyle replaced him with Wregget once again. The Moose went on to lose, but they bounced back with a tight defensive effort the following night to even the series.

It was another low-scoring contest in Game 3 back at the Arena, but Wregget's shoddy goaltending cost the Moose once again as they lost 2-1.

"The Moose did carry the territorial edge throughout the game, but were unable to overcome their coach's decision to name Ken Wregget the starting goaltender. The mystifying decisions to continue to play Wregget have cost the Moose many games this season, and it did again on this night. Both Aeros goals came from long range, but somehow eluded Wregget,"[14] was how I summed up the game.

The game-winner came on a lazy drifter from the point that sailed past Wregget. Rather than simply step to one side and block the shot with his big frame, he dove at it like a soccer goalie trying to cover a net as wide as the entire rink.

Oddly, in his article on the game the following day, Tim Campbell would call it a "sizzling"[15] shot. Perhaps he was just trying to be diplomatic, but the description was laughably inaccurate. A good number of the fans in the stands could likely have shot the puck just as hard.

The fact that Wregget stiffened his legs and dove at that shot suggested he had an injury that kept him from bending to one side. For his sake, I hoped he was indeed injured, which would explain why he missed a shot, not unlike so many others he had whiffed on, that he surely would have handled with ease earlier in his career.

Salajko started Game 4 and gave his team adequate goaltending, but the normally ultra-reliable Brian Chapman's uncharacteristic giveaway in overtime sent the Moose down to a heartbreaking 3-2 defeat.

"The Moose did have more opportunities during the game, but a combination of [Aeros goaltender Frederic] Chabot and their own ineptitude cost them dearly,"[14] as I wrote after the game.

Facing elimination in Game 5, Carlyle again turned back to Wregget, his favorite toy, to save the season. I fumed as I watched Wregget lead the Moose out to start the game, but he turned in his best outing of the season, and Jimmy Roy's rebound goal in the second overtime gave the Moose a dramatic victory that sent the series back to Houston.

Having seemingly discovered the Fountain of Youth, the Moose's modern-day Ponce de Leon was spectacular in both games in Houston. The Moose won Game 6 in another double-overtime thriller, then took Game 7 to complete the improbable comeback from the brink of oblivion and advance to the next round.

Wregget's miracle revival continued as the Moose earned a split of the first two games of the Western Conference Final in Chicago against their old and all-too-familiar foes. Tempers flared late in Game 2 and several players were ejected late in the third period. The ruckus continued off the ice, and Chris LiPuma of the Wolves was alleged to have made a threat involving a firearm, a charge that LiPuma would deny.

Back at the Arena for Game 3, Wregget was again strong, and Dan Kesa's flip shot over perennial nemesis Wendell Young in overtime gave the Moose another sudden-death victory. The Moose now had their arch-rivals on the ropes, but as compelling as this freakish playoff run was becoming, this Cinderella story would not have a fairytale ending.

Wregget reverted to his regular-season form the following night, and the Wolves evened the series with a convincing victory. Former Moose goaltender Richard Shulmistra blanked his former team 1-0 in Game 5 to put the Moose on the brink of elimination once again as the series shifted back to Winnipeg for Game 6.

The Moose jumped out to a 4-1 lead and looked to have the game well in hand before an epic third-period collapse ended their season in a most inglorious fashion with a 6-4 defeat. After the game, Brett Hauer was nearly in tears when describing the play on the Wolves' third goal when the puck took an awkward bounce off the glass and caught Wregget out of position.

The Wolves celebrate after winning Game 6.[1]

The handshake line.[1]

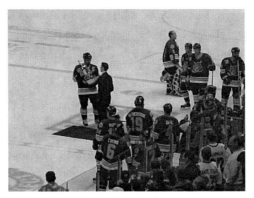

Steve Maltais accepts the Western Conference championship trophy.[1]

While the Moose could only wonder what might have been, the Wolves advanced to the finals against Orlando. The Solar Bears quickly dispatched the Wolves in five games to take what would be the IHL's last championship. The clock had struck midnight not only for the Cinderella Moose but also for the entire league. A new era in the history of top-tier minor-league hockey was about to dawn.

The Other Side of the Mountain

Only a week after the Orlando Solar Bears celebrated their Turner Cup championship, the IHL announced it was closing up shop, confirming rumors that had been circulating for the past several months.

> After 56 years, the International Hockey League announced today that it was dissolving effective October 1, 2001. Although the dissolution effective date is October 1, 2001, the IHL will cease day-to-day operations and begin winding up its affairs immediately. This announcement comes as a result of a board of governor's meeting that was held via conference call on Friday June 1. The future of each of the league's member teams will be announced in the coming days and weeks.

> "It is with great sadness that I make this announcement," said IHL President and CEO DOUGLAS G. MOSS. "With the landscape of minor league hockey continuing to evolve, the league's board of governors determined that this was a necessary decision. On behalf of everyone in the IHL and all those that have come before us, we thank our many fans for their loyalty and support throughout the years and urge them to continue to support the greatest sport in the world at both the major and minor league levels."[1]

Six of the IHL's 11 remaining teams, including the Moose, would join the rival AHL. The other five, including the IHL's last champions, would either fold or join lower-level minor leagues.

That same day, I listened in on the teleconference involving Mark Chipman and other principals in the deal. Among the items discussed was that, at Chipman's insistence, the Moose were being placed in the same division as the AHL's other Canadian teams. Nearly all those teams, however, against whom the Moose would play more than a third of their games, were located at the extreme eastern edge of the continent. With many of the Moose's former IHL rivals so much closer geographically, the move made no sense whatsoever.

The increased and needless amount of travel would put the Moose at a tremendous competitive disadvantage, to say nothing of the extra travel costs despite the comparative strength of the U.S. dollar. Chipman, however, managed to finagle a deal to have the AHL cost-share travel expenses among all its teams.

I would come to deeply resent Chipman's attempt to force-feed me with his handpicked set of opponents. As a fan, I felt like I was being told what to do, and on strong principle, I would categorically refuse to attend games involving those teams.

The following day, at the invitation of Kristy Nykoluk, my account representative, I attended the press conference at the Arena to formally announce both the Moose's move to the AHL and their new affiliation with the Vancouver Canucks.

Master of Ceremonies Don Wittman addresses the gathering.[1]
Seated from left to right are Randy Carlyle, Stan Smyl, Brian Burke, Mark Chipman, David Andrews and David Nonis.

Since AHL teams could dress only six veteran players, and with nearly all the quality young players in the game with NHL organizations, it was virtually impossible to continue operating as an independent team. The Moose needed an NHL affiliation and signed a five-year deal with Vancouver.

Randy Carlyle's position as the coach was the sticking point in previous negotiations, and Chipman was forced to capitulate and allow the Canucks to appoint Stan Smyl as the Moose's new coach. Utterly devoted and loyal to his subordinates, Chipman was not going to leave Carlyle without a job and named him the nominal club president.

Though the title sounded impressive, with the Canucks in charge of the hockey operations and Chipman handling the business end, the position would offer few challenges for Carlyle. He would leave the nest a year later to take a position as an assistant coach with the Washington Capitals. Assistant coach Scott Arniel, another Chipman favorite, was allowed to remain and would work alongside the Canucks' Barry Smith in assisting Smyl.

Stan Smyl.[1]

Smyl was one of the most ornery players to ever lace up a pair of skates and always seemed to be in ill humor on the ice. At the press conference, however, he showed a much different side. He was exceptionally gregarious and personable and even cracked a joke, pointing to a spot along the boards behind him where he first met Carlyle and "exchanged a few F words."

Smyl commanded much respect as a player, but unfortunately, the same would not hold true as a coach. Far too often, his teams would simply go through the motions and give less than a representative effort, and as a result, the Moose remained a bottom-feeder under Smyl. Though Carlyle's persona was heavily overblown in the local media, he was at least able to command the respect of his team, and the Moose rarely lost because they were outworked.

Following his third season with the Moose, Smyl rejoined the Canucks front office and would never hold another coaching position in the pros. Much to Chipman's delight, the Canucks agreed to bring Carlyle back the following year. After one season, however, Carlyle would again leave the nest, this time for Anaheim, where he would spend the next seven seasons as the Ducks' head coach.

After the Ducks' championship in 2007, Chipman was so proud of his former subordinate that he would place a picture of Carlyle holding the Stanley Cup on the Moose's billboard ads all around Winnipeg.

The Canucks would delight Chipman once again when they appointed Arniel as the Moose's head coach in 2006. Armed with a plethora of top prospects from a revamped Canucks organization, the Moose would enjoy much success under Arniel, including a trip to the Calder Cup finals. Following four years with the Moose, Arniel would leave the nest for an ill-fated season and a half with the dreadful Columbus Blue Jackets of the NHL.

Also at the press conference, the Moose debuted new uniforms along with a third jersey modeled after the Canucks' dark blue sweaters.

Randy Carlyle, Stan Smyl and Brian Burke model the Moose's new jerseys.[1]

The new home whites and road greens featured the removal of the angled stripe along the bottom, replaced by a more traditional look. The Canucks' logo was also placed on the left shoulder of all three jerseys.

As part of ever-increasing ties to the military, the Moose would later introduce special military-themed jerseys that they would wear on special occasions.

Tyler Bouck wearing the military-themed uniform.[1]

In the coming years, the Moose would alter their look once again when they cast aside one of the most popular logos in the game, replacing it with what looked like the face of a wounded bear trying to twist its foot out of a trap.

Jimmy Roy in the Moose's new duds.[1]

It was the cartoonish moose that first drew me to the team, and I was crushed to see that original logo so cavalierly discarded. In 2008, *The Hockey News* ranked the new logo highly, but at 11th of 29 AHL teams, it was a major step down from the top spot the original logo enjoyed for so long.

The affiliation would see the Canucks supply most of the players for the Moose, leaving most of last year's roster to find work elsewhere in the AHL or in Europe. Only captain Brian Chapman, Jimmy Roy and Justin Kurtz would remain with the Moose for this coming season. Even Cory Cyrenne, who had become something of a sacred cow because of his Manitoba heritage, was among the many cut adrift.

Ken Wregget and Mike Ruark both retired, and Rusty Fitzgerald, the team's leading goal scorer, followed a path familiar to IHL players by signing to play in Germany. Unfortunately, Fitzgerald again soon fell victim to the injury bug, which put an end to his career.

Sean Pronger surprisingly stuck in the NHL with Columbus for a full season before signing with the Canucks organization and a second go-round with the Moose. Mel Angelstad signed with the Capitals organization and was eventually rewarded for his dedication and perseverance when Washington promoted him for a pair of NHL games.

Mel Angelstad with the Portland Pirates.[1]

While in one of those games with the Capitals, Angelstad challenged veteran tough guy Sandy McCarthy to a scrap, but McCarthy declined the invitation, leaving Angelstad without an NHL fight to his credit.

Finally free from the Oilers' clutches, Brett Hauer signed with the Los Angeles Kings, who subsequently traded him to the Nashville Predators. Sadly, he would get into only three more NHL games and would finish his star-crossed career with stints in Switzerland and Russia.

Hauer would be the last recipient of the Larry D. Gordon Trophy as the IHL defenseman of the year, yet it was Chapman who was quite rightly named the Moose's best defenseman in their annual end-of-season awards. It was perhaps only fitting that the IHL's last defenseman of the year was not even the best blueliner on his own team.

Kurtz would play for the Moose for two more years. Often a healthy scratch and a part-time resident in Carlyle's doghouse since coming to the Moose, he would shockingly earn a call-up this coming season and play in 27 games for the Canucks.

Chapman would remain the Moose's captain and anchor their blue line for the next two years before the Moose blindsided him with his release just a month before training camp.

Tim Campbell of the *Free Press* spoke with him afterwards and had this to say about their conversation:

"Chapman, half-sounding like he hadn't gotten the licence plate of the moving truck that had just flattened him, was at a loss for words when reached at his Springfield, Mass. home yesterday."

"When I left town, Zinger [Craig Heisinger] had indicated to me that they were interested in having me back. I'm not really sure what happened," said Chapman. "Am I surprised at what happened? Well, a little bit. Kind of the way I left it leaving town, I was kind of expecting to be back next season."

"I've got nothing on the table now, nothing definite. I'll keep plugging away. If, at the end of last season, I had known, I could have had my name out there. Now some of the jobs are already filled."[2]

"Chappy's [Chapman] paid great dividends here and I would never diminish anything he's done. But with the young defense we're going to have, I thought all things being equal, the job [veteran defenseman] Dallas [Eakins] was doing in Chicago helping young players, he was better suited for that job than Chappy was," said Heisinger. "Maybe Chappy deserved the opportunity, but I didn't feel we had the luxury to wait to find out."

"Chappy is first and foremost my friend."[2]

With friends like that, Chapman didn't need any enemies.

"All those words in August don't do justice to what the Moose fairly owe Chapman for his years of stability and leadership,"[2] said Campbell in summing up this tawdry affair.

Indeed, no one in franchise history handled himself with more class on and off the ice than Brian Chapman. He had earned the right to go out in a similar fashion, and I was appalled to see how ghoulishly his release was handled. In all my years as a passionate sports fan, I had never been so embarrassed to be a fan of a team as I was with the Moose. I wanted to put a match to my Moose jersey.

Fortunately, Chapman would hook up with the Rochester Americans before the start of the season, and I would be there to see him when he came back to face the Moose.

Brian F. Chapman with the Rochester Americans.[1]

Roy would play another five seasons for the Moose and be their last remaining player from the IHL era. He finished his career as an IHL alumnus should, with a stint in Germany. He would eventually return to Winnipeg and work for Chipman in the front office of his NHL team.

With the move to the AHL, Chipman and the Crocus Fund purchased the 50% stake in the team held by Kevin MacLean, thus ending the franchise's last remaining ties to Minnesota.

The increased connection to the NHL brought a little more attention to the Moose, but it wasn't translating into increased attendance. Crowds continued to dwindle, and the Arena was between a third and half full on most nights. Rather than devote some attention to the waning fan interest, Chipman turned his focus to the construction of his new downtown arena.

Looking to sell seats in the new building, Moose ticket representatives began stationing themselves by the front doors before games. Out of curiosity one night, I approached the desk and perused a seating plan. The Moose representative then began his sales pitch, encouraging me to buy a season ticket or mini-pack because "you might miss out."

With so few people at the games, it amazed me that he could say such a thing with a straight face. I nearly laughed in his face, but instead I replied, "I'll take my chances."

Moose hockey would never become a hot ticket and it was only the novelty of the new building that would draw crowds. I would hear stories about fans buying mini-packs just to get first dibs on tickets in the event that Chipman was successful in his efforts to acquire an NHL team.

On the ice, since the AHL was also just one level below the NHL, I naively assumed there would be few differences between the AHL and IHL. AHL hockey would be faster paced and arguably slightly higher quality than the IHL, but the experience following an AHL team would prove to be quite different from following an independent IHL club.

I would feel a much stronger attachment to the IHL players than I would ever feel about those in the AHL. The veteran-laden IHL became a lightning rod for critics, who would call the league hockey's equivalent of an old folks' home, but those players were ours, so to speak, and not someone else's.

I might have felt differently if I were a Canucks fan, but since I wasn't, I would find it increasingly difficult, if not impossible, to cheer for their players. It felt akin to going to another city to cheer on my team's arch-rival. It was not nearly as much fun, and it was one of the most significant reasons that my interest in the team began to fade.

In the IHL, rosters were almost entirely rebuilt from season to season, but in the AHL, more players would stick for longer periods of time. Call-ups to Vancouver during the year, however, would make the in-season roster a virtual revolving door. The coasties would be no less important to the Moose than they had been in the IHL as they filled the holes in the lineup most admirably.

The new type of Moose player – younger, more eager and with the allure of being a future NHL star – would also draw a new type of fan. Female admirers young and old would flock to the rink and swoon over some of these players, much like Fiona Quick, who, years earlier, was infatuated with Parris Duffus to the point of obsession.

Unquestionably, the most popular Moose player among these puck bunnies was Canucks prospect Pat Kavanagh. A former second-round draft choice of the Philadelphia Flyers, Kavanagh had been toiling in the Canucks organization for many years. The Canucks had called him up on occasion and he got into a couple of NHL games, but he was at best a marginal player. Even with the Moose, he was little more than a depth player, and though he was a good penalty killer, it became difficult to understand why the Canucks were wasting their time with him. He clearly had no future in the NHL.

Pat Kavanagh.[1]

Those details, however, were of little importance to his many "fans." Tall and good looking with long, wavy black hair that fluttered in the wind, "Kavy," as he was affectionately called, sent hearts racing with every stride. No doubt, he could have starred in a remake of the movie *Fatal Attraction.*

"He works *so* hard," was a familiar refrain among his legion of puck bunnies. He did work hard. He just wasn't very good.

Three of his most ardent admirers would religiously camp out before the doors opened, then make a beeline for the ice and wait for the warm-up to begin.

Pat Kavanagh's legion of "fans."[1]

In this trio, there was one teenage girl trailing behind two adults in their late 30s or early 40s. One of the adults would often be wearing a Moose jersey with the nameplate "KAVANAGH" and his number 15 emblazoned on the back, but often worn with the back turned out front pressed against the glass.

Keenly aware of where his admirers were, Kavanagh would make a point of skating past them at least once during the warm-up and flicking his hair in their direction. Each time he skated by, they were so awestruck by his presence that I expected each one of them to faint.

On the rare occasions in which Kavanagh actually scored a goal, from their seats high up in the north end, they would leap to their feet in a fit of unbridled joy and send a shrill that would echo around the largely empty Arena. I suspect none of them got any sleep on those nights.

Initially, I found this spectacle humorous, but as time went on, I began to see it as the sad, pathetic sight that it was. It is behavior I would have more expected out of lovestruck teenagers rather than grown, supposedly mature adults.

I can only imagine the pain they endured when the Canucks finally jettisoned Kavanagh, thus depriving them of their cherished idol.

Kavanagh also had his share of supporters online. Perhaps his most fervent online "fan" went by the handle of "Czarina" on the Moose's official online message board. In her many posts, she would gush over his every move and endlessly praise her choice as the Moose's hardest-working player.

I was not one to check this board often, but by sheer accident, I happened to visit when the Moose had just switched their board over to a new system, requiring all existing users to re-register. Sensing an opportunity to drive "Czarina" batty, I quickly registered that handle for myself using an anonymous e-mail address.

Just as I had suspected, "Czarina" threw a hissy fit and went as far as to complain to the webmaster to see if she could get her handle back. After getting nowhere with him, she finally settled on the new handle of "HockeyCzarina" and continued right where she left off in espousing her devotion to "Kavy." In the meantime, however, I have no doubt that I caused her a few sleepless nights.

Interestingly, a regular poster who went by the handle of "Hollywood" was sometimes accused of being me. I did post on rare occasions, but never under that handle.

Canucks prospect Tyler Bouck did not have a flock of admirers like Kavanagh, but his one staunchly loyal "fan" more than made up for the lack of numbers. Lisa Williams of Dallas would regularly send me e-mails asking for updates on Bouck as well as pictures of him. I was happy to oblige initially, since Bouck had once played for the Dallas Stars, a team I had followed closely ever since the Jets left Winnipeg. Lisa would respond in kind with some pictures from Stars games she had attended.

Tyler Bouck.[1]

In one of her many e-mails, Lisa proudly told me about how she got "attached" to Bouck when he got his first taste of the NHL with the Stars before being traded to Vancouver. Her fandom seemed somewhat normal for a time until she told me about her plans to fly to Houston to stake out Bouck and the Moose at their hotel.

She also grew increasingly frustrated as Bouck was increasingly relegated to penalty-killing duties and had his ice time reduced. She snapped at me when I once dared to suggest that Bouck may not be an NHL-caliber player.

Lisa was clearly much more than just a "fan" and I soon broke up our e-mail exchanges. Though he wouldn't get much of a shot with the Canucks, Bouck may not have known how fortunate he was to have left Dallas and his most fanatical supporter.

Despite the numerous differences between the two leagues, fighting would be no less important in the AHL than it was in the IHL. Having younger and less mature players in the AHL would also make for more intense battles that would occasionally get out of hand. As an example, during a fight in November 2002, Darcy Verot would try to gouge out Bouck's eye, earning him a two-game suspension and a lifetime of scorn from Lisa.

Zenith Komarniski.[1]

After the Moose's entry into the AHL, a mural went up near the airport depicting players from each of Winnipeg's three pro sports teams. It would perhaps not be an accident that Zenith Komarniski was chosen as the Moose's representative on the mural, since he would have the honor of becoming the first AHL Moose player to get involved in a fight.

These early years in the AHL, though not nearly as much fun, would also provide a smattering of colorful characters and indelible moments. In addition to Kavanagh and Bouck, goaltender Alex Auld was one of the most unforgettable characters.

Alex Auld.[1]

Auld was a highly regarded prospect in the Canucks organization who would go on to enjoy a long, though not spectacular, career in the NHL. Tall, lean, unusually bald for someone of his tender age and secretively aloof, Auld was perhaps best known as the one player most uncomfortable with fans and specifically with children, the organization's preferred demographic.

My friend Steve would regularly bring his young son, Paul, to the annual Moose Sports Carnival as well as to other events where players would be attending. While almost all the other players, Jimmy Roy in particular, were more than accommodating, Auld kept his distance from Paul and the other children. In the shooting gallery, instead of letting him score, Auld was blocking Paul's shots as if it were Game 7 of the Stanley Cup Final. Paul would quickly adorn Auld with the moniker "Stinky Alex."

When I wrote about "Stinky Alex" in a column on my Web site, rather than being apologetic, Jeff Mager, the Moose's director of community relations, fired off a snarky e-mail to me, staunchly defending Auld.

Auld would also seemingly operate with dual personas as he shuttled between the Moose and the Canucks. With the Moose, he would be called "Alexander," whereas in Vancouver, he would go by "Alex." The changeover would remind me of a scene in the Arnold Schwarzenegger movie *True Lies*, when Schwarzenegger's character switched over from being a secret agent to a computer salesman.

As part of a routine that he had obviously long since perfected, he madly switched passports and other documents as well as slipped on a wedding ring. I could imagine Auld doing something similar in an airplane heading in or out of Winnipeg as he swapped his Alexander and Alex identities.

Years later, when I traveled to the Xcel Energy Center in Saint Paul to see the Stars for the first time in 13 years, I was less than pleased to see none other than "Stinky Alex" playing goal for Dallas.

Though there would be little passion in Winnipeg for the Moose, there was plenty to be had for the AHL in other cities. On one occasion, a group of particularly dedicated fans flew in from Providence to watch their Bruins battle the Moose in a pair of weekend games. One of them had even posted on the Moose's message board days in advance asking fans for recommendations on hotels and restaurants.

I was dumbfounded when I saw them sitting high up in the nosebleed seats. Their view was made even worse by the newly installed netting, the ridiculous brainchild of NHL commissioner Gary Bettman regrettably copied in the AHL. These fans had undoubtedly spent a king's ransom to fly halfway across the continent, to say nothing of their expenses for hotels and meals, only to scrimp on the few extra dollars it would have taken to get better seats. It was a display of foolish frugality that would have made many Winnipeggers, known nationwide for that very quality, immensely proud.

My last Moose game came in March 2004, and I would never again follow their fortunes. Over the coming years, I would occasionally be offered free tickets and decline each time. I longed for what the Moose were during their years in the IHL, not what they had become.

My experiences with Chipman and seeing how things are run off the ice has taken the fun out of being a fan. I cannot watch games with the same unbridled passion I once had and pro sports is no longer a dominant part of my life.

I would miss the many humorous and off-the-wall experiences and all the colorful characters that came along with the ride. As I had expected, the quality of play was well below NHL standards, but I felt a greater part of Moose hockey than I had ever felt being a Jets fan.

Before the Jets left, I used to think the hockey world began and ended with the NHL. Following the Moose made me realize the NHL is but a small part of that hockey world, a world that has so much more to offer than I could have ever realized. I once used to look down on the minor leagues and feel sorry for fans who were supposedly stuck with nothing better. Today, I envy those fans.

"It was the best 15 years of my life,"[3] said longtime fan Mike Delaney.

Following 10 seasons in the AHL, the Moose moved to St. John's, Newfoundland, to make way for the NHL. Using funds from David Thompson, one of the richest men in Canada, and the Manitoba government, Chipman acquired control of the Atlanta Thrashers in 2011 and moved them into his new arena. Reluctantly acceding to the wishes of the overwhelming majority of Winnipeg hockey fans, he would rebrand the team as the "Winnipeg Jets." Four years later, he would move his AHL franchise back to Winnipeg for a second go-round, with the two teams sharing the same home rink.

A popular urban legend says the Moose survived for 15 seasons in Winnipeg because of their ownership, but in reality, they survived in spite of it. Ever since the team's move from the Twin Cities in 1996, the Moose were badly neglected by an organization that felt it was entitled to support without having to earn it.

The Moose brand, once such a hot commodity, is today poisoned and damaged beyond repair. Many fans are genuinely embarrassed to be seen in Moose paraphernalia and Mike Delaney is regularly chastised for wearing his Moose jacket to a so-called Jets game.

There is perhaps no more fitting epitaph for a team as unwanted as any in the history of the game.

Bibliography

Calgary Sun, "The uncivil war: Calgary @ Edmonton," Eric Francis, September 3, 2003, http://www.canoe.ca/Slam030919/col_francis-sun.html

Conversation with Mike Delaney, October 11, 2012

The Fanhub, "Top 10 Most Dysfunctional Sports Franchises," http://fanhub.me/posts/detail/379465/Top-10-Most-Dysfunctional-Sports-Franchises

DropYourGloves.com, January 19, 1996 Game Report, http://dropyourgloves.com/fights/GameEvents.aspx?Game=94527

Fort Wayne News Sentinel, October 8, 1997

Hockeydb.com

Hockey-fights.com, "Larry Shapley," March 2004

The Hockey News, AHL Logo Rankings, August 4, 2008, http://www.thehockeynews.com/articles/17449-THNcoms-AHL-Logo-Rankings.html

Kelowna Daily Courier, September 13, 2006, http://www.kelownadailycourier.ca/article_524.php

Manitoba Moose brochure, "Team Builder Program"

Manitoba Moose letters to season ticket holders: February 25 and April 28, 2000

Manitoba Moose Media Guide: 1996-1997, 1997-1998, 1998-1999, 1999-2000, 2000-2001, 2001-2002

Midwest Sports Channel, television broadcast, December 31, 1995

moosefans.com Game Notes, 1996-2001

Niagara Falls Review, February 2012

Orlando Sentinel, November 20, 1997

Plaidworks.com IHL mailing list archive

The Province, January 15, 1999

QB Court Registry, http://jus.gov.mb.ca/

Robinson for the Defense, Larry Robinson, Chrys Goyens (McGraw-Hill, 1988)

Star Tribune, December 6, 1994

24 Hours, CBC interview with Mark Chipman, aired September 28, 1998

Valentinedesign.net

Wikipedia.org
http://en.wikipedia.org/wiki/Greg_Pankewicz
http://en.wikipedia.org/wiki/Dan_Snyder

Winnipeg Free Press
January 1979: 18
August 1995: 17
September 1995: 26, 27
November 1995: 29
December 1996: 4, 6, 7, 8
February 1996: 24

March 1996: 9, 10

April 1996: 30

May 1996: 1, 2, 3, 5, 15, 16, 17, 18, 22, 24

July 1996: 2, 5, 9, 24

August 1996: 29

September 1996: 15, 16, 17, 18, 19, 20, 21, 22, 23, 24, 25, 26, 27, 28, 29

October 1996: 1, 2, 3, 4, 5, 6, 7, 8, 9, 10, 11, 12, 13, 16, 17, 18, 19, 20, 21, 22, 23, 24, 25, 26, 27, 28, 29, 30, 31

November 1996: 1, 2, 3, 4, 6, 7, 8, 12, 13, 14, 15, 16, 17, 19, 20, 21, 22, 23, 24, 26, 27, 28, 29, 30

December 1996: 1, 2, 3, 4, 5, 6, 7, 9, 10, 11, 12, 13, 14, 15, 16, 17, 18, 19, 20, 21, 22, 23, 24, 27, 28, 29, 30, 31

January 1997: 2, 4, 5, 6, 7, 9, 10, 11, 12, 13, 14, 15, 16, 18, 19, 20, 22, 23, 24, 25, 26, 27, 28, 29, 30, 31

February 1997: 1, 2, 3, 4, 5, 6, 7, 8, 9, 10, 11, 12, 13, 14, 15, 18, 19, 20, 21, 22, 23, 25, 26, 27, 28

March 1997: 1, 2, 3, 4, 5, 6, 7, 8, 9, 10, 11, 12, 13, 14, 16, 18, 19, 20, 21, 22, 23, 24, 25, 26, 27, 29, 30, 31

April 1997: 1, 2, 3, 4, 5, 6, 7, 8, 9, 10, 11, 12, 13, 14

June 1997: 4, 10

September 1997: 5, 13, 14, 15, 16, 17, 18, 19, 20, 21, 22, 23, 25, 26, 27, 30

October 1997: 1, 2, 3, 4, 5, 6, 7, 8, 9, 10, 11, 12, 14, 15, 16, 17, 18, 19, 21, 22, 23, 24, 25, 26, 27, 28, 29, 30, 31

November 1997: 1, 2, 3, 4, 5, 6, 7, 8, 9, 10, 12, 13, 14, 15, 16, 17, 18, 19, 20, 21, 22, 23, 24, 25, 26, 27, 28, 29, 30

December 1997: 1, 2, 3, 4, 5, 6, 7, 8, 9, 10, 11, 12, 13, 14, 15, 17, 18, 19, 20, 21, 22, 27, 28, 29, 30, 31

January 1998: 2, 3, 4, 5, 7, 8, 9, 10, 11, 12, 14, 15, 16, 17, 18, 19, 21, 22, 23, 24, 25, 26, 27, 29, 30, 31

February 1998: 1, 2, 3, 4, 5, 6, 7, 8, 9, 10, 11, 12, 13, 14, 15, 16, 17, 18, 19, 20, 21, 22, 23, 25, 26, 28

March 1998: 1, 2, 3, 4, 5, 6, 7, 8, 9, 11, 12, 13, 14, 15, 16, 17, 18, 19, 20, 21, 22, 23, 24, 25, 26, 27, 28, 29, 30, 31

April 1998: 1, 2, 3, 4, 5, 6, 8, 9, 11, 12, 14, 15, 16, 17, 18, 19, 20, 21, 22, 23, 24

June 1998: 13

September 1998: 11, 19, 21, 22, 23, 24, 25, 26, 27, 28, 29, 30

October 1998: 1, 2, 3, 4, 5, 6, 7, 8, 9, 10, 11, 13, 14, 15, 16, 17, 18, 20, 21, 22, 23, 24, 25, 26, 27, 28, 29, 30, 31

November 1998: 1, 3, 4, 5, 6, 7, 8, 10, 12, 13, 14, 16, 17, 18, 19, 20, 21, 22, 23, 24, 26, 27, 28, 29, 30

December 1998: 1, 2, 3, 4, 5, 6, 7, 8, 9, 10, 11, 12, 13, 14, 15, 16, 17, 18, 19, 20, 21, 22, 23, 26, 27, 28, 29, 30, 31

January 1999: 2, 3, 4, 6, 8, 9, 10, 11, 12, 13, 14, 15, 16, 17, 21, 22, 23, 24, 25, 26, 27, 28, 29, 30, 31

February 1999: 3, 4, 5, 6, 7, 8, 9, 10, 11, 12, 13, 15, 17, 18, 19, 20, 22, 24, 25, 27, 28

March 1999: 1, 2, 4, 5, 6, 7, 8, 9, 10, 12, 13, 14, 15, 17, 18, 19, 20, 22, 23, 24, 25, 26, 27, 28, 29, 30, 31

April 1999: 1, 3, 4, 5, 6, 7, 8, 9, 10, 11, 12, 13, 14, 15, 16, 17, 18, 19, 20, 21, 22, 23, 24, 25, 26, 27, 28, 29, 30

May 1999: 1, 2, 3

September 1999: 11, 14, 15, 16, 17, 18, 19, 20, 21, 23, 24, 25, 26, 27, 28, 29, 30

October 1999: 1, 2, 3, 4, 5, 6, 8, 9, 10, 13, 14, 15, 16, 17, 18, 19, 20, 21, 22, 23, 24, 26, 27, 28, 29, 30, 31

November 1999: 2, 3, 4, 5, 6, 7, 9, 10, 12, 13, 14, 15, 17, 18, 19, 20, 21, 23, 24, 25, 26, 27, 28, 29, 30

December 1999: 1, 2, 3, 4, 5, 6, 8, 9, 10, 11, 12, 13, 14, 15, 16, 17, 18, 20, 21, 22, 23, 28, 29, 30, 31

January 2000: 2, 3, 4, 5, 6, 7, 8, 9, 10, 12, 13, 14, 15, 16, 18, 19, 20, 22, 23, 24, 25, 26, 28, 29, 30, 31

February 2000: 1, 2, 3, 4, 5, 6, 7, 8, 9, 10, 11, 12, 13, 14, 15, 16, 17, 18, 19, 20, 22, 23, 24, 25, 26

March 2000: 1, 2, 3, 4, 5, 6, 7, 8, 9, 10, 11, 14, 15, 16, 17, 18, 19, 21, 22, 23, 24, 25, 27, 28, 29, 30, 31

April 2000: 1, 2, 3, 4, 5, 7, 8, 9, 11, 12, 13, 14, 15, 16, 17, 18, 19, 20, 23, 25

September 2000: 12, 18, 19, 20, 21, 22, 23, 24, 26, 27, 28, 29, 30
October 2000: 1, 2, 3, 4, 5, 6, 7, 8, 10, 11, 12, 13, 14, 15, 16, 17, 18, 19, 20, 21, 22, 23, 24, 26, 27, 28, 31
November 2000: 1, 2, 4, 5, 6, 7, 9, 10, 12, 13, 15, 16, 17, 18, 19, 20, 21, 24, 25, 26, 27, 28, 29, 30
December 2000: 1, 2, 3, 5, 6, 7, 8, 9, 10, 11, 12, 13, 14, 15, 16, 17, 18, 19, 20, 21, 22, 23, 24, 26, 28, 30, 31
January 2001: 2, 3, 4, 5, 6, 7, 9, 10, 11, 12, 13, 14, 15, 16, 17, 18, 19, 20, 21, 22, 23, 24, 25, 26, 27, 28, 31
February 2001: 1, 2, 3, 4, 5, 6, 7, 8, 10, 11, 12, 13, 14, 15, 16, 17, 18, 20, 21, 22, 23, 24, 25, 26, 27, 28
March 2001: 1, 2, 3, 4, 5, 6, 8, 9, 10, 11, 12, 13, 14, 15, 16, 17, 18, 19, 20, 21, 22, 23, 24, 25, 26, 27, 28, 29, 30, 31
April 2001: 1, 2, 4, 5, 6, 7, 8, 9, 10, 11, 12, 14, 15, 16, 18, 19, 20, 21, 22, 23, 24, 25, 26, 27, 28, 29, 30
May 2001: 1, 2, 3, 4, 5, 6, 7, 8, 9, 10, 11, 12, 13, 14, 15, 16, 17
June 2001: 4, 5, 6
June 2002: 20
November 2002: 24, 27
August 2003: 7
July 2004: 21
October 2013: 5

Winnipeg Jets: The WHA Years Day by Day, Curtis Walker (PCMP Press, 2013)

Winnipeg Sun
October 1996: 5
November 1996: 9, 10, 11
March 1997: 14, 16
February 1998: 26, 27, 28
October 1999: 10
February 2000: 12

Notes and Credits

Into the Abyss

1. *WFP*, May 5, 1996
2. Valentinedesign.net

1996-1997: The First Season

1. *WFP*, May 2, 1996
2. *WFP*, May 5, 1996
3. *WFP*, July 9, 1996
4. *WFP*, December 4, 1996
5. *WFP*, September 15, 1996
6. *WFP*, September 22, 1996
7. *WFP*, December 2, 1996
8. plaidworks.com IHL list archive
9. *WFP*, September 27, 1996
10. *WFP*, October 25, 1996
11. *WFP*, October 31, 1996
12. *WFP*, November 7, 1996
13. *WFP*, December 6, 1996
14. *WFP*, September 29, 1996
15. *WFP*, January 25, 1998
16. *WFP*, January 12, 1997
17. *WFP*, December 12, 1996
18. *WFP*, December 31, 1996
19. *WFP*, January 11, 1997
20. *WFP*, January 10, 1997
21. *WFP*, February 13, 1997
22. *WFP*, February 1, 1997
23. *WFP*, February 2, 1997
24. *Robinson for the Defense*
25. *WFP*, February 7, 1997

26. *WFP*, February 2, 2000
27. QB Court Registry
28. The Fanhub, "Top 10 Most Dysfunctional Sports Franchises"
29. *WFP*, February 27, 1997
30. *WFP*, February 28, 1997
31. DropYourGloves.com
32. *Calgary Sun*, September 3, 2003
33. *Kelowna Daily Courier*, September 13, 2006
34. Rob Gialloreto e-mail, October, 1999

1997-1998: Spinning Wheels

1. *WFP*, April 17, 1997
2. *WFP*, June 10, 1997
3. *WFP*, April 9, 1997
4. *Niagara Falls Review*, February 2012
5. *WFP*, September 5, 1997
6. 24 Hours, Mark Chipman interview, aired September 28, 1998
7. *WFP*, September 25, 1997
8. *WFP*, September 30, 1997
9. *WFP*, October 5, 2013
10. moosefans.com Game Notes
11. *WFP*, November 17, 1997
12. *WFP*, October 17, 1997
13. *Orlando Sentinel*, November 20, 1997

14. *WFP*, December 2, 1997
15. *WFP*, January 2, 1998
16. *WFP*, April 14, 2001
17. *WFP*, March 11, 2001
18. *WFP*, February 5, 1999
19. *WFP*, January 8, 1998
20. *WFP*, February 6, 1998
21. *WFP*, February 21, 1998
22. *WFP*, March 3, 1998
23. *WFP*, March 25, 1998
24. *Star-Tribune*, December 6, 1994
25. *WFP*, October 9, 1998
26. *WFP*, April 24, 1998

1998-1999: False Dawn

1. *WFP*, September 27, 1999
2. *WFP*, October 20, 1998
3. moosefans.com Game Notes
4. *WFP*, November 4, 1998
5. *WFP*, November 5, 1998
6. *WFP*, March 19, 1999
7. *WFP*, November 13, 1998
8. *WFP*, November 30, 1998
9. *WFP*, December 22, 1998
10. *The Province*, January 15, 1999
11. *WFP*, February 3, 1999
12. *WFP*, April 3, 1999
13. *WFP*, April 27, 1999
14. *WFP*, May 1, 1999

1999-2000: Crash Landing

1. *WFP*, September 11, 1999

2. *WFP*, September 24, 1999
3. *WFP*, October 1, 1999
4. Hockey-fights.com, "Larry Shapley," March 4, 2004
5. *WFP*, November 2, 1999
6. *WFP*, November 17, 1999
7. *WFP*, November 20, 1999
8. *WFP*, November 29, 1999
9. *WFP*, February 18, 2000
10. *WFP*, December 12, 1999
11. *WFP*, December 30, 1999
12. Moose letter to season ticket holders, February 25, 2000
13. *WFP*, April 16, 2000
14. *WFP*, April 25, 2000
15. *WFP*, April 3, 2000

2000-2001: The End of an Era

1. Moose letter to season ticket holders, April 28, 2000
2. *WFP*, January 17, 2001
3. *WFP*, October 26, 2000
4. *WFP*, January 22, 2001
5. *WFP*, October 2, 2000
6. CJOB radio interview, November 11, 2000
7. *WFP*, November 30, 2000
8. *WFP*, January 2, 2001
9. *WFP*, February 13, 2001
10. *WFP*, March 13, 2001
11. *WFP*, March 23, 2001
12. *WFP*, March 30, 2001
13. *WFP*, January 18, 1979
14. moosefans.com Game Notes

15. *WFP*, April 27, 2001
16. *WFP*, March 17, 2001

The Other Side of the Mountain

1. IHL Press Release
2. *WFP*, August 7, 2003
3. Conversation with Mike Delaney, October 11, 2012

Photos

1. Author's collection.
2. Handout at Winnipeg Jets game, March 1996.
3. Invoice from Manitoba Moose, June 2, 1996.
4. Mike Delaney's collection.
5. RoamingTheRinks.com.
6. Published on wikipedia.org under the Creative Commons Attribution 3.0 Unported license by Leech44.
7. Stan Milosevic's collection.
8. Published on Wikimedia Commons by Arnold C (User:Buchanan-Hermit).
9. Manitoba Moose ticket stub from Select-A-Seat, November 20, 1998.
10. Published on wikipedia.org under the Creative Commons Attribution 3.0 Unported license by Scorpion0422.

About the Author

Born and raised in Winnipeg, Manitoba, Curtis Walker lives in St. Catharines, Ontario. He is an avid historian of both the original (1972-1996) Winnipeg Jets and the World Hockey Association and a member of the WHA Hall of Fame advisory board.

This is his fourth book. His first book, *Winnipeg Jets: The WHA Years Day by Day*, is available both electronically and on paper through the WHA Hall of Fame at www.whahof.com.

His second book, *My Journey with Carli*, detailing his experience with Carli Ward, a 25-year-old who passed away of cervical cancer, is available in paperback at www.createspace.com/4453527 and electronically at www.amazon.com/dp/B00IAYJSXI. Read more about Carli's story at www.carlislegacy.net.

His third book, *Coming Up Short, The Comprehensive History of the NHL's Winnipeg Jets (1979-1996)*, is available in paperback at www.createspace.com/4613701 and electronically at www.amazon.com/dp/B00IAVGRTY.

Visit the author's Web site: curtiswalker.com
Follow the author on Twitter: @curtisw72

CPSIA information can be obtained at www.ICGtesting.com
Printed in the USA
LVOW06s1256120715

445931LV00033B/1313/P